AF229509

The Power of Prayer

The principles of prayer made easy and understandable for practical application

Olivia Daniels Pierce

authorHOUSE®

AuthorHouse™
1663 Liberty Drive, Suite 200
Bloomington, IN 47403
www.authorhouse.com
Phone: 1-800-839-8640

First published by AuthorHouse 9/24/2007

ISBN: 978-1-4343-2100-8 (sc)

Printed in the United States of America
Bloomington, Indiana

This book is printed on acid-free paper.

Special Dedication

I would like to dedicate this book to the loving memory of my mother, Mrs. Lorene Daniels and my sister, Joann Huggins, who has always believed in me, encouraged me, and gave me the strength to believe in myself. In the year 2005, God called them to receive their heavenly rewards; however, their prayers will forever cover and guide me. Also, this book is dedicated to my children, who supported and graciously tolerated me as I relentlessly requested that they read and reread, as I wrote. In the winter of 2006, God called my father, Mr. Leo Daniels home to heaven. Thank you, Dad, for your nurture and support all the years that you took care of me. Thank you for the love and the treasure of wisdom you planted in my life.

Special Thanks

First of all, I give thanks to our Lord and Savior Jesus Christ for being the passion of my life and the lover of my soul. I would like to thank my pastor, Pastor Louvenior Dewitt, for being a great servant of God. Pastor Dewitt, you are a woman of godly wisdom and a great inspiration in my life. Because of your impartations in my life, my faith and foundations in Christ are stable. I would like to thank Dr. Charles Randall of Saint Delight Ministry, my instructor who was there for me during some difficult times. I love and appreciate him very much for all that he's instilled in my life. I would like to thank Dr. Johnell Rowell for all of your support and for the famous saying "Write it down." Also I would like to give my deepest appreciation to Elder Lasonya Reaves for all the patience and time that you took going over my book. You're the best. A special thanks to my children, Heath and Vaccarol Reaves, Regina, Melissa, Danielle, and Mekel, who have supported and encouraged to continue to write. I'd like to give a special thanks to all of my brothers, Sgt. Ariel Daniels, Earl, Ryndia, and S.G. Daniels and my sisters Sgt. Loretta Daniels, Assistant Pastor Equilla Long, and Evangelist Mary Long for their love, support, and faith in my abilities through Christ Jesus. I love you all very much. I couldn't dare leave out my two special daughters that God placed in my life Abbigail Bellamy and Rose Marie Gerald that supported me in the publishing of this book. Thank You!

CONTENTS

Introduction

As I began to write this book, it was my desire to reveal the power, purpose and the necessity of prayer especially in the life of the believer. I realized that there are a variety of types, forms, and methods of prayers; therefore, it's not my intention to attempt to categorize each of them. At best, my goal is to simplify what prayer is! In addition, I desire to provide a clear understanding of the abilities of prayer and provide some straightforward techniques for teenagers and those who are babes in Christ without taking away from the importance and power of prayer. Moreover, I desire to reveal the significance of our role in creation and the authority that was given to us as God's visible representatives in earth.

When we read about Jesus, His purpose, the miracles, signs, and wonders that were performed by Him while He was in the flesh, it seems that our finite minds still can't begin to comprehend the full measure of the pain and suffering He endured in being the ultimate sacrifice, and the perfect sin offering. Whether we believe it or not, we are programmed to always recognize Him as the begotten Son of the Father; therefore, we tend to picture Him more in his deity than in his humanity. Throughout this book, I wish to introduce Jesus as Mary's son who walked the earth in complete humanity.

Although Jesus was sin free, he was able to feel pain just like you and me! He felt the tearing of his skin during the scourging and piercing of the nails as they were driven into his hands! He didn't divest himself of His deity, but He withheld His preincarnated glory and in humility, voluntarily restricted use of his divine power and became one of us.

While having a conversation with a group of teenagers about prayer and listening to what they had to say, I was really amazed to know most of them felt the same way I did when I was younger. They felt that they did not know how to pray properly. Whenever they had to pray, they were at lost for the right words. I began telling them that there really are no right words to say because prayer is simply talking to God from your heart and allowing Him to speak back to you through His word and in your spirit. However, there is an order in which we should enter into His presence. We should always enter into His presence with praises of thanksgiving, adoration, and acknowledging God as our Father.

Around age thirteen, I had confessed Christ. Immediately, I was told that it was time for me to learn to pray. My family consisted of nine children, my mom, and my dad. In my parents' home, we always had family prayer. Each time we had prayer, my father would appoint one of us to pray. By doing this he was trying to make sure that we learned to reverence God and to instill spiritual values within us. Finally, it was my time to pray. Even after hearing and witnessing my family members praying, it seemed very hard for me because I was busy trying to think of things to say.

I had always heard people praying, but their prayers seemed so formal and neatly put together. I remember listening to some of the older people as they prayed in church. Some of them had those neatly fitted prayers which they had prayed for so long that when they got up to pray, I could almost recite their prayers word for word before they even said anything. After becoming an adult, I began seeking the Lord because I desired to have a personal relationship with Him. It was then I realized prayer was not about saying a lot of eloquent and enticing words carefully connected. Those types of prayers were patterned prayers, which were memorized and had no significance.

However, prayer is talking to God from your heart! It is making your petition known to Him, giving Him praise, and adoration for who He is, what He's done, and what He's still doing in your life. Prayer is the way in which we pour out our souls to God in order to reveal our inner most thoughts. He is not looking for the person who can recite vain, artificial words at the snap of a finger. God is looking for the individual, who will cry out to him their your heart and soul, in complete submission seeking to know him. God is looking for people who are willing to surrender themselves completely to his will. He's looking for a yielded vessel that will allow his glory to be revealed in the earth through them.

One of the youngsters in the group made a statement that he prayed every night before going to bed. Another teen replied, "Yeah, all you say is the Our Father Prayer." As I begin to think about that, I said, "That's good because that is actually all you would need to say if you understand its revelation". At that point, I began telling them my opinion of our model prayer revelation. He along with the others thought that this actually made praying a lot simpler to do.

As I explained to them, prayer is so simple that even the smallest child can pray; yet, at same time it is the highest and holiest work done by us. It is through prayer our souls are given birth into the kingdom of God. When we pray, the powers of the eternal world

have been placed at our disposal. Through prayer, we receive the
secret powers of abundant life and open the channel through which
all our blessings flow.

WHAT IS PRAYER?

In biblical terminology, prayer is calling on God and asking for the things that we desire whether spiritual or temporal. It is also designed so that we can put God to work in human or world affairs on earth. Without prayer, man is a mere creature of circumstances, left at the mercy of blind fate. This leaves man with the great responsibility of the sorrows, burdens, and afflictions of life without any source of resolution. For the believer, prayer should be a lifestyle of constantly staying in the presence of God expressing continuous gratitude, to Him for who He is, what He has done, and what He is still doing in our lives. Prayer is talking with God and listening for God to speak back to us in our spirit as we yield ourselves to Him. Even though we know that God is omniscient, or all knowing, there are still some important factors in receiving anything from God.

All we have to do is ask, seek, and knock (Matthew 7:7). In Isaiah 45:11-12, God compels us to ask of Him the things that we desire of him.

> Thus said the Lord, the Holy one of Israel, and His
> Maker, ask me of the things to come concerning my

> sons, and concerning the work of my hands command
> ye me. I have made the earth and created man upon
> it: I, even my hands, have stretched out of the heavens,
> and all their hosts I have commanded.

It is necessary to realize that when God made man he gave man complete authority on earth and free will to make choices. As a result, God will not override our will. In order for God to intervene in our human affairs, we have to ask or give Him permission. Ask, and it will be given unto you; seek, and you shall find; knock and the door shall be opened (Matthew 7:7, Luke 11:9-13). This lets us know that in order to receive the things we desire from God it is necessary to ask. Even though He knows our thoughts before we think them, God still allows us the opportunity to make choices and decisions concerning our lives. To grant us *things* because He wishes us to have them would infringe upon our right of free will. In other words, God would be enforcing his will and taking away our ability to choose. Therefore, I say to you whatever things you ask for when you pray, believe that you will receive them and you shall have them (Mark 11:24). Once we ask of him, we must, in faith, believe that we will receive the things we request. After all God is our father who loves us unconditionally and our petitions are important to Him. When we go to our earthly parents with a request if it is within their power to fulfill it, they will.

> If they know how to give good gifts to us being of
> an evil nature, how much more will our father in
> heaven give good things to those who ask? And this
> is the confidence that we have in Him that, if we ask
> anything according to His will, He hearth us: And if
> we know that He hears us, whatsoever we ask, we know

that we have the petitions that we desired of Him (I John 5:14-15).

Now, that we have asked, our next step is to seek God. But, how? We seek God is through reading his word to know His will and through prayer. We seek to hide His truths, which is his word, deep into our hearts. This is why David said, "Thy word have I hid in mine heart, that I might not sin against thee" (Psalms 119:11). When seeking God, we must be persistent in our search to know him. Then shall ye call upon me, and ye shall go and pray unto me, and I will hearken unto you. And ye shall seek me, and find me, when you seek me with all your heart (Jeremiah 29:12-13).

Even in being persistent, it is important to come before his presence in humility. For about how you see yourself, admit that you need God's help! As we seek him he reveals himself to us through his word and His spirit. In Matthew 6:33, He compels us to seek first the kingdom of God and His righteousness and whatever things we desire will be added to us.

At times, we have asked God for request and find that we did not receive. It is not because God was not able but because we asked amiss. We did not have the faith to believe we would obtain our request. Moreover, there are times we ask believing we are asking according to His will and it seems our requests go unanswered. Still, it's not that God was not able but our request may not be His will for us. Our thinking is so small and narrow we tend to limit what God can actually do. We are looking at something small when it is God's will to give us something grand. Ephesians 3:20 states, "Now unto him that is able to do exceeding abundantly above all that we ask or think, according to the power that worketh in us". Therefore, believe in God's ability to do the impossible (See Matthew 19:26).

Sometimes when we ask for things it is also important to consider the timing. We have to realize timing is very important with God (See Ecclesiastes 3:1). There are times that we are not in the right place in life, or in Him, for God to grant the petition that we requested. If He releases what we've asked, it may cause us hardship, or cause us to make spiritual error. For example, there are times that our children will ask us for things such as cars, or to do other things that we feel as parents that they are not responsible enough to handle. If we go against our instinct and release these things to them, it could be a very costly mistake. If we wait until they are mature enough to handle what they are asking for they stand a better chance of being able to handle what ever it is that they desire. There are circumstances that put us into different situations to refine us spiritually. The reason for this is so that the eyes of our understanding is enlightened; that we may know what is the hope of His calling, and what are the riches of the glory of His inheritance in us.

Although prayer is communicating with God, it is also where we disrobe ourselves of all pretense and artificiality telling God our most intimate thoughts and desires. Our words must be heartfelt and coming from the depths of our souls, not just memorized patterns using eloquent and enticing words. We must come before Him in complete submission acknowledging our imperfections and desiring His perfection. Prayer is the strongest link between God and man because it purifies the air and destroys the powers of darkness (Colossians 1:13) Prayer gives us the right to take hold of God and His strength (Colossians 1:11).

Since prayer is the first step in getting to know the Lord Jesus, for the sinner, this prayer must be a prayer of repentance. A sinner must acknowledge to God that he is a sinner and ask to be forgiven of all sins. Confessing with his mouth and believing with his heart that Jesus is the Son of God, and that God raised Him from the dead. For with the heart one believes unto righteousness, and with the mouth confession is made unto salvation (Romans 10:9-10). Therefore salvation is a change of the heart, but after you have confessed Him in sincerity at some point the spirit will give witness. The Spirit itself [bears] witness with our spirit, that we are the children of God (Romans 8:16). When we receive salvation, our thoughts and desires change and we began to look at life from a different view. II Corinthians 5: 17 declares that when we are saved through Christ we have become new creatures and old things have passed away, behold all things have become new. This means that the things that you use to indulge in that are not of Christ, you should no longer indulge in because you know that it is not the right way. As you began to refrain from or *cut loose* from the things that are not like Christ the very God of peace will sanctify your heart. As you pray and seek the presence of God He will give you His strength that will enable you to walk in the newness of life. John 5:24 says that we have passed from death to life, meaning that because we are the offspring of Adam's seed, we were born in sin with a death sentence on our lives. Now after we are saved through the spirit of Christ who has already made atonement for our sins we are reborn into eternal life through him. We have been transferred from the rule of darkness to the Kingdom of God's Son (Colossians 1:13). As a result, we are no longer bound by the chain and burden of sin but made free through the sacrifice of Jesus Christ.

> For as by one man's disobedience many were made
> sinners, so by the obedience of one shall many be made
> righteous.

> Moreover the law entered, that the offence might
> abound. *But where sin abounded, grace did much more
> abound*:

> That as sin hath reigned unto death, even so might
> grace reign through righteousness unto eternal life by
> Jesus Christ our Lord (Romans 5: 19-21).

Where sin once had rule and dominion over us, the grace, the favor, and the love of God abounded much more, thus freeing us and enabling us to walk as children of light.

Prayer takes hold of God and influences Him to work for us. God has placed Himself under the law of prayer to the extent that He is induced to work among people that pray. Because prayer puts God to work on earth by the same token prayerlessness prevents His ability to work for us. As Christians, we are to recognize our dependence upon God, His unlimited love, His atoning provisions at the cross, His resurrection, and His continuing presences in our lives through the Holy Spirit. Prayer meets the inner needs in our lives and teaches us to trust God for directions and instructions.

Prayer strengthens our souls, builds our faith in God, gives us freedom from fear, and fosters inward peace. Through prayer we receive, power to live holy, deliverance from strongholds, power to witness, and power speak the word of God with boldness. God grants us wisdom and understanding of the knowledge of His word through prayer (James 1:5 and 2Timothy 3:16-17). The word of God is vital to your prayer life because it is the very essence of who God is. Everywhere in His word, prayer shapes God's actions and attitude. God makes prayer identical in force and power with Himself. When you pray speaking God's word back to him, He will respond to it because this is what he identifies himself as; therefore, His word is a promise with power that is infallible. As you pray consistently with His word and you are aligned with the word, there are guaranteed results. In John 15:7, Jesus put Himself at our command in prayer when He said that if you abide in me, and my words abide in you, you shall ask what you desire and it *"shall"* be done. Through prayer, we open the door for God to move in the earth realm. God gave man the authority to have dominion and reign here in the earth realm. Yet, He designed it so that man would have to ask of Him in order for Him to intervene in earthly situations. By asking, we give Him the legal right to move. He is not imposing his will on us but simply carrying out request. In simpler terms, He is just doing what you asked him to do.

As people of God, when we pray we carry God's purpose by releasing him to work in our lives so that He can reign on earth. He said that whatever is needed for his cause, ask him, and he would do it. God binds Himself to our prayers. Because God's purpose and plans are hinged on prayer, it is prayer, which obligates Him to move. James 5:16 states that the effectual fervent prayer of a righteous man [avails] much.

When we pray, our prayers build walls of protection around our families, community, state, and even our nation as a whole. 2 Chronicles 7:14

If my people, which are called by my name, shall humble themselves, and pray, and seek my face, and turn from their wicked ways; then will I hear from heaven, and will forgive their sin, and will heal their land. I believe that righteous prayers are so powerful they transcend time to protect coming generations, as noted here in Joshua 24:1-17. Using Joshua as a mouthpiece, God reminds Israel of his loyalty, compassion, and unfailing power. Because their predecessors petitioned God and believed, the nation of Israel was delivered and sustained.

THEN JOSHUA gathered all the tribes of Israel to Shechem, and summoned the elders of Israel and their heads, their judges, and their officers; they presented themselves before God.

Joshua said to all the people, Thus says the Lord, the God of Israel, Your fathers dwelt in olden times beyond the Euphrates River, including Terah the father of Abraham and Nahor, and they served other gods.

And I took your father Abraham from beyond the Euphrates River and led him through all the land of Canaan and multiplied his offspring. I gave him Isaac,

And I gave to Isaac Jacob and Esau. And I gave to Esau the hill country of Seir to possess, but Jacob and his children went down to Egypt.

I sent Moses and Aaron, and I plagued Egypt with what I did in the midst of it; and afterward I brought you out.

I brought your fathers out of Egypt, and you came to
the sea; and the Egyptians pursued your fathers with
chariots and horsemen to the Red Sea.

When they cried to the Lord, He put darkness between
you and the Egyptians, and brought the sea upon
them and covered them; and your eyes saw what I did
in Egypt. And you lived in the wilderness a long time
[forty years].

I brought you into the land of the Amorites who lived
on the other side of the Jordan; they fought with you,
and I gave them into your hand, and you possessed
their land, and I destroyed them before you.

Then Balak son of Zippor, king of Moab, arose and
warred against Israel, and sent and called Balaam son
of Beor to curse you.

But I would not listen to Balaam; therefore he blessed
you; so I delivered you out of Balak's hand.

You went over the Jordan and came to Jericho; and the
men of Jericho fought against you, as did the Amorites,
Perizzites, Canaanites, Hittites, Girgashites, Hivites,
and Jebusites, and I gave them into your hands.

I sent the hornet [that is, the terror of you] before you, which drove the two kings of the Amorites out before you; but it was not by your sword or by your bow.

I have given you a land for which you did not labor and cities you did not build, and you dwell in them; you eat from vineyards and olive yards you did not plant.

Now therefore, [reverently] fear the Lord and serve Him in sincerity and in truth; put away the gods which your fathers served on the other side of the [Euphrates] River and in Egypt, and serve the Lord.

And if it seems evil to you to serve the Lord, choose for yourselves this day whom you will serve, whether the gods which your fathers served on the other side of the River, or the gods of the Amorites, in whose land you dwell; but as for me and my house, we will serve the Lord.

The people answered, Far be it from us to forsake the Lord to serve other gods;

For it is the Lord our God Who brought us and our fathers up out of the land of Egypt, from the house of bondage, Who did those great signs in our sight and preserved us in all the way that we went and among all

the peoples through whom we passed. Amplified Bible
Joshua 24: 1-17

As noted in the history of the children of Israel, prayer to God allowed the defeat of their enemy and sustained the lives of their families. When we use prayer as a secondary force in our lives, we are limiting God's ability to work effectively in our lives, or circumstances. Little praying or poor praying weakens God's power on earth, postpones the glorious results of His reign, and retires God from His sovereignty here on earth. To know His will and to experience His glory are both tied to prayer. Throughout the history of man, God's greatest manifestations as evident in our greatest revivals, such as the Asusa Street Revival, were and still are conditioned by the force of prayer. Without a consistent, faithful, prayer life, man cannot expect to see the full manifestation of the manifold wonder of God!

Prayer Gives Us Power to Live Holy

As I use the term power to live holy, this simply does not mean you become perfect immediately when you receive the Holy Spirit. You have to realize that living holy is not just something you can categorize in a small box or package because it covers a multitude of things. Living holy comes through a process of time as you pray and seek the presence of God. When you receive the Holy Spirit, he empowers you and gives you the strength and the ability to trust God to the point that He can transform your life. But you shall receive power after that Holy Spirit has come upon you (Acts 1:8). The more you are in God's presence praying and seeking him, he gives you his strength, to lay aside or separate from worldly desires and live according to all He has commanded.

And be not conformed to this world: but be ye transformed by the renewing of your mind, that ye may prove what is that good and acceptable, and perfect, will of God (Romans 12:2).

When I was younger the older saints in the church would always tell us that once we were saved, we had it made. They would say to us, you don't have to worry any more about anything. They made it seem as if the battle was over, but I can assure you that they were wrong to some extent. Although we have already been given complete victory over satan this does not stop his challenges. Actually, now that you are saved you have just become a threat to Satan as well as an enemy, so the battle or struggle has now really just begun. Satan does not want you be saved; therefore, he is really going to try and wreck your life in every way possible. Now, you have put on Christ and are strengthened with might through His spirit, in your inner person (See Roman 13: 14). God has also empowered us through the word of God, which is our weapon to win the battle. The word in the hands of the believer is the most powerful weapon because it transforms our lives, situations, and circumstances.

> For the word of God is quick and powerful and sharper
> than any twoedged sword, piercing even to dividing
> asunder of soul and spirit, and of the joints and
> marrow,and is a discerner of the thoughts and intents
> of the heart (Heb 4:12).

As we pray, our prayer goes up before God as a sweet odor of incense and brings God into the atmosphere to save, to bless, and to work wonders. When God's work flourishes His kingdom triumphs in earth. As we pray our prayers build up barriers against the powers of evil and destroy them so that the ministry in us and in our churches will become more effective.

> For though we walk in the flesh, we do not war after
> the flesh:

> For the weapons of our warfare are not carnal, but
> mighty through God to the pulling down of strong
> holds;

> Casting down imaginations, and every high thing
> that exalteth itself against the knowledge of God, and
> bringing into captivity every thought to the obedience
> of Christ (II Corinthians 4:3-5)

As a result, our prayers have to be grounded in the word of God. It is the word of God that provides us with the confidence to stand firm knowing that he has already given us victory in the every battle. As we pray and seek the face of God, He strengthens us according to his glorious power to endure all our tests with patience and longsuffering. Moreover, He provides us with joy, an overwhelming sense of happiness and contentment that does not change because of test or trial.

After you have accepted Christ as your personal savior, it is necessary to seek to be filled with or baptized in the Holy Spirit so that you will be empowered to witness the gospel of Jesus Christ. The Holy Ghost is Jesus Christ living inside of you!

> And they were all filled with the Holy Ghost, and
> began to speak with other tongues, as the Spirit gave
> them utterance (Acts 2:4).

> But the Comforter, which is the Holy Ghost, whom
> the Father will send in my name, he shall teach you
> all things, and bring all things to your remembrance,
> whatsoever I have said unto you (St. John 14:26)

> But when the Comforter is come, whom I will send
> unto you from the Father, even the Spirit of truth,

> which proceedeth from the Father, he shall testify of
> me (St. John 15:26)

> Nevertheless I tell you the truth; It is expedient for you
> that I go away: for if I go not away, the Comforter will
> not come unto you; but if I depart, I will send him
> unto you. John 16:7

Through the power of the Holy Spirit and the authority in the name of Jesus, you can storm the gates of Hell and win souls, which will help to enlarge the kingdom of God.

When we pray earnestly before God, we have all of heavens power at our disposal. Prayer affects three different spheres of existence: the divine, the angelic, and the human. It puts God to work, which is the divine, it puts angels to work, which is the angelic, and it puts humans to work, which brings the forces of heaven into play on earth. Through prayer Jesus will give you power to overcome any challenge that is before you. In Psalms 46:10, He tells us to be still and know that He is God. We are to stand still, holding firmly to our faith and know that we have already conquered every situation that arises. According to I Peter 5:8, we are to be sober, meaning (responsible) and vigilant, meaning (watchful, or careful) because our adversary the devil, as a roaring lion, walketh about, seeking whom he may devour. Take notice, that the word of God is careful to always say *"as"* a roaring lion, and not *"is"* a roaring lion. Most of us, we read *as a roaring lion* and mentally create the image of the lion, an animal known to be ferocious. Thusly, we project this image onto the devil. By using the word "like", Peter gave us a reason not to fear. The word "like" implies that Satan is portraying himself to be something he is not. Even Satan all the demonic forces know that they are truly powerless. How can I make such a bold statement? Because James 2:19 plainly states that the devils believe in God and tremble.

I am not trying to discredit his ability to be cunning, deceptive, and crafty schemer in any way. For the Bible tells us, we are not ignorant of his devices (II Corinthians 2:11). Yet, as Christians, we must see through his disguise. Fear is the tool he uses to cripple and blindside us. True, he has some ability but *GREATER* is the power of Jesus!

> And Jesus came and spake unto them, saying, All power is given unto me in heaven and in earth (Matthew 28:18).

> Wherefore God also hath highly exalted him, and given him a name which is above every name:

> That at the name of Jesus every knee should bow, of things in heaven, and things in earth, and things under the earth;

> And that every tongue should confess that Jesus Christ is Lord, to the glory of God the Father (Philippians 2:9-11).

By giving ourselves over to Christ and submitting to His will through the word of God, Satan has no power over us. The only power Satan can have is power we give to him.

Unlike God, Satan is not omnipotent. He only has the power over your actions that you give him. When Christ rose from the grave, He rose with all power in His hands. Therefore, He is not only *all* powerful. He is *all* power!

Roman 13:14 tells us to put on the Lord Jesus Christ. If we do this, we too have all power (meaning Christ). Salvation brings us back into right standing with God but the indwelling of the Holy Ghost empowers us to defeat Satan and take authority over every scheme that he has planned against any area of your life. This is why Isaiah 54:17, states that no weapon that is formed against you shall prosper. This is your heritage as being a servant of the Lord. As we pray, we are to be clothed with the whole armor of God that we will be able to stand against the wiles of the devil.

For this reason, you will have to stand having your loins girt about with the truth, which is to have your mind filled with the word of God. Your mind is the door through which the spirit of God enters. Having on the breastplate of righteousness, allows the truth of God's word to be conceived in your heart. The breastplate of righteousness shields your heart from the fiery darts of the devil. Why a breastplate? During times of war, soldiers wore heavy amour to protect the vital organs. A direct wound to the heart would immediately kill the solider. If your heart is not shielded, you are easily dismayed and discouraged.

The shield is symbolic of the protection God provides to give him time to transform you! In order for you to be a representative of Christ on earth, he has to be sure you will talk like him and act like him! Through his word, Jesus speaks into your heart.

When the heart has been transformed it will have an effect in your walk and your daily actions. You should be taking the shield faith that you maybe able to quench the fiery darts of the wicked, and know for your self that in Christ you are more than a conqueror. The Christian life is a struggle that requires decision and effort simply because we are still living in fleshly bodies. The helmet of salvation to serves as a shield for the mind. As Christians, we must maintain balance and stability. Throughout our Christian walk, we may be faced with false teaching or instances of spiritual error. We have to know how to handle these situations without being confused. We are guided through these situations through prayer.

Although learning the methods of praying is simple enough, the battle comes in the application. To effectively develop a prayer life, one has to devote his time. Spending time in prayer is costly and difficult. Not only must you deny yourself of natural pleasures such as going shopping or having lunch with friends at your time of prayer, you must content with spiritual forces of evil ruled by the devil. The Gospel of Luke gives a vivid account of the power of prayer. Because Jesus was in a human body, he felt pain and agony. However, he demonstrated that by connecting to our heavenly Father through prayer God will provide us with supernatural strength to carry out any assignment or task. When it comes to prayer, there will be a withdrawing from those who you hold dear. To press into the heavenly power of God, it takes effort. It takes energy and time!

> And he was withdrawn from them about a stone's cast, and kneeled down, and prayed,

> Saying, Father, if thou be willing, remove this cup from me: nevertheless not my will, but thine, be done.

> And there appeared an angel unto him from heaven, strengthening him.

And being in an agony he prayed more earnestly: and his sweat was as it were great drops of blood falling down to the ground. (Luke 22:1-44)

Just as Jesus labored in prayer, there are times when you will have to be persistent and press your way into the presence of God. You will have to be like Jacob to some extent. Jacob is remembered because he "wrestled" or "waged war" in prayer.

And Jacob was left alone, and a Man wrestled with him until daybreak.

And when [the Man] saw that He did not prevail against [Jacob], He touched the hollow of his thigh; and Jacob's thigh was put out of joint as he wrestled with Him (Amplified Bible Genesis 32:24-25)

By refusing to let go until he received a blessing, Jacob's character, not just his name, was changed forever.

Then He said, Let Me go, for day is breaking. But [Jacob] said, I will not let You go unless You declare a blessing upon me.

[The Man] asked him, What is your name? And [in shock of realization, whispering] he said, Jacob [supplanter, schemer, trickster, swindler]!

And He said, Your name shall be called no more Jacob [supplanter], but Israel [contender with God]; for you have contended and have power with God and with

men and have prevailed (Amplified Bible Genesis
32:26-28)

The persistency of prayer changes not only situations and circumstances but the individual as well!

Still, there will be times when the forces around you will try to hinder your breakthrough succumb. Our spiritual enemies are not made of flesh and blood but are supernatural beings of evil controlled by Satan. These beings are the rulers of darkness of this age that have blinded the eyes, ears, and minds of the world of unregenerate people, to the spiritual values of God and His will. These forces are not all powerful and through prayer God will give us adequate power to subdue them. You have to understand that God does not give us victory without our full commitment to him and our best effort in earnest prayer. This is why it is necessary to know that your life is hidden in Christ and you have been made conformable to His death. Psalms 91:1 states "He that dwelleth in the secret place of the most high shall abide under the shadow of the Almighty". Furthermore, David goes on to validate his state in Psalms 27:2 by recalling times God had protected and delivered him out of hands of his enemies. David's total confidence is in the Lord. Because of his belief in prayer, David is confident that God will *not* fail to rescue him when he calls (See Psalms 27:5). How do we know this? David uses the word *shall.* The term shall express the inevitable, or better yet, the expected.

When the wicked came against me to eat up my flesh,
my enemies and foes, they stumbled and fell (Psalm
27:2)

For in the time of trouble, He shall hide me in His pavilion. In the secret place of His tabernacle He shall hide me (Psalms 27: 5).

As we pray, the powers of darkness are destroyed. We gain power to access to spiritual blessings in heavenly places that we need for salvation and to live Godly lives. We are His workmanship created so we can do the good works that He had planned for us from the beginning. Ephesians 1:4 states "God had chosen us in him before the foundation of the world, that we should be holy and without blame before him in love". You have not chosen me, I have chosen you, and ordain you that you should go and bring forth fruit (John 15:16). It is time for us to rise and become the Sons of promise and the daughters of destiny that God had preordained us to be, going forth in Christ taking the kingdom of God by force with the word of God and prayer. Staying before God in prayer opens a never-ending channel of strength. When the flesh, the sin nature, desires to rise, God's power will stand up. The power of God gives you the authority to call your flesh subject to the will of God. Therefore, you are able to exercise restraint with ease and not with a struggle.

Living holy is a non-stop process, which will continue in us until our departure from this life. If you will submit yourself to Him in complete dedication desiring to know Him, God will reveal himself to you. For so long we have been lead to believe that our intimacy with God was up to Him. This is not the case. Your true level of intimacy with God is up to you. It is you who will determine how close you walk with Him. You will be the determining factor in deciding how much you are willing to sacrifice for God's purpose to be fulfilled in your life. Although salvation is free, it is not cheap.

It is free because it is a gift from God that does not cost us anything. At Calvary, Jesus paid the price for our freedom.

> For there is one God, and one mediator between God and men, the man Christ Jesus;

> Who gave himself a ransom for all, to be testified in due time (Timothy 2:5-7)

Even as the Son of man came not to be ministered unto, but to minister, and to give his life a ransom for many (Matthew 20:28).

Jesus bridged the gap between God and man. Now that the way has been open for us all, the only cost to you is acceptance and the surrendering of your soul to God. People often wonder how to repay their debt to Jesus Christ. Believe me, one could never hope to repay such a debt. However, to answer this question, your willingness to sacrifice your soul to unto God is a start.

The soul realm is synonymous with your emotions. It is the area where your emotions are located and where your most challenging battles will be fought. One of our greatest fights stem from hurt. In a sense, we refuse to accept the fact we have to endure some hardship. For a Christian, our pain may stem from rejection by loved ones, loss to death, or even our own denial of personal desires. Emotional pain, unlike physical pain, cannot be eased with medication. Because we like instant gratification, we want relief from our pain quick, fast, and in a hurry! When it comes to the healing of emotional pain, it takes time.

In our Christian walk, the emotional pain received leaves invisible scars.

The scars may be the results of spiritual growth. Throughout my Christian walk, I recall the older saints telling us *if you can't carry a cross you, can't wear a crown.* As a Christian, our only recourse is to prepare for emotional pain. In order to reign with Christ, we must suffer with Him. In Isaiah 53:2-12, we find that Jesus was despised and rejected of men; a man of sorrows and acquainted with grief; smitten of God and afflicted.

> Yet it pleased the Lord to bruise Him; when thou shalt
> make his soul an offering for sin, he shall see his seed,
> he shall prolong his days, and the pleasure of the Lord
> shall prosper in his hands (Isaiah 53:10).

In order to live holy, you must purpose in your heart to present your body a living sacrifice holy and acceptable unto God, which is your reasonable service (Romans 12:1). For the perfect will of God to manifest in our lives, we have to be willing to make our souls a sacrifice. You have to be willing to lay aside every weight and the sin that would so easily beset you (Hebrews 12:1). Ungodly actions and ways must not be a part of our Christian lives. Living holy is a way of life.

Holy living calls for a transformation of our thinking. The apostle Paul clearly tells us to be transformed by the renewing of our minds (Roman 12:2). In addition, Peter instructs us to "be sober, and watch unto prayer"; meaning be (responsible) and seek God in prayer (I Peter 4:7). Then, as God promised, he will reward you by revealing his purpose for your life (See Hebrews 11:6).

> Having made known to us the mystery of his will,
> according to his good pleasure, which he had purposed
> in himself (Ephesians 1:9).

As you read his word and take heed to it you will began to take off the corruptible things of this world and put on the incorruptible things of God (Daniel 1:8). In the bible, we find Daniel was carried away to Babylon while he was a young man. But because he believed God, he had purposed in his heart not to be defiled by the Babylonians culture. Although Daniel faced many challenges in his time, God always brought him out victoriously because he was a man of prayer. When you purpose in your heart to live for God, as you pray, God gives you his strength and as you read the word, it is the weapon that empowers you to fight the good fight of faith and trust God. Even though the outward man is perishing, the inward man is being renewed day by day. God's word is your written contract or will. Without fail, God watches over it to perform it.

> Look to Me and be saved, all the ends of the earth! For
> I am God, and there is no other.

> I have sworn by Myself, the word is gone out of
> My mouth in righteousness and shall not return
> (Amplified Bible Isaiah 45:22-23)

Seek God In Prayer To Know Your Purpose

In order to be effective in any area of life, you must know your purpose. As you pray and seek the Lord, He will reveal your purpose. Once you know your purpose, you need to have a pattern or blueprint for your life.

> And the LORD answered me, and said, Write the
> vision, and make it plain upon tables, that he may run
> that readeth it.
>
> For the vision is yet for an appointed time, but at the
> end it shall speak, and not lie: though it tarry, wait
> for it; because it will surely come, it will not tarry
> (Habakkuk 2:2-3).

Take notice that the scripture does not give *the time* of manifest but *assures* us of manifestation. Even though you may not see the promises and prophecies being manifested at the present time, be patient and steadfast for they will come to pass.

As you pray and seek the Lord, a relationship will form. Over time as you learn to trust Him more, he will direct your steps.

Just as there is a period of courtship in any relationship, there is a courtship period in the development of your relationship God. This is why he tells us to "learn of him" (Matt. 11:29). During your period of courtship you are getting to know God, and God is preparing you for your purpose. He is equipping you with the spiritual tools you will need to be His spokesman, or an effective witness of the gospel. It is impossible for you to represent someone effectively unless you have spent quality time with them.

According to Matthew 20:16, "many be called but few chosen". To be a member of the "chosen", you have to study, be trained, and disciplined by God. The Bible tells us to be aware of false prophets and false doctrines.

> Because strait is the gate, and narrow is the way, which leadeth unto life, and few there be that find it.

> Beware of false prophets, which come to you in sheep's clothing, but inwardly they are ravening wolves.

> Ye shall know them by their fruits. Do men gather grapes of thorns, or figs of thistles? (Matthew 7:14-16)

> And many false prophets shall rise, and shall deceive many (Matthew 24:11).

> Now the Spirit speaketh expressly, that in the latter times some shall depart from the faith, giving heed to seducing spirits, and doctrines of devils;

Speaking lies in hypocrisy (I Timothy 1:1-2).

Those who are chosen spend time with God through prayer. In prayer, you seek the presence of God. The more you enter into his presence the more of your "flesh" has to die. Paul wrote, "I die daily (I Corinthians 15:31)", in order to take on the characteristics of Jesus Christ. Paul asserts that through this study of Christ his greatest desire is to be like Jesus! In Philipians 3:14, Paul states, "I press toward the mark for the prize of the high calling of God in Christ Jesus". The prize "is to be like Christ"! If you are like him, then, you can effectively represent him in the earth. Therefore, you are willing to allow him to shear or cut away the corruptible things in your life.

You have to ask and allow him to circumcise your heart and renew your mind. It's necessary to spend time with Him in prayer and reading His word. The application of biblical truths to your life is your way to victory. Do not be content to feel His spirit, but learn to walk and live in it daily so that He may order your steps. Psalms 37:23 says that the steps of a good man are ordered by the Lord. The trust you have built in Him brings an indescribable, overwhelming peace. You have an unshakeable certainty that God will perform whatever he has told you. The struggle of wondering if God will or will not is over! Your mindset is centered on the fact that God has the power to create and bring those situations, which seem to work against, obedient to his will. If you have allowed God to have control over you and in you, the power God has, you have! You can "call those things which be not as though they were (Romans 4:17).

> For though we walk in the flesh, we do not war after the flesh:

> (For the weapons of our warfare are not carnal, but
> mighty through God to the pulling down of strong
> holds;)
>
> Casting down imaginations, and every high thing
> that exalteth itself against the knowledge of God, and
> bringing into captivity every thought to the obedience
> of Christ (2 Corinthians 10:3-5).

Our view must change from looking at everything in the natural sense. We do not look at the things which are seen but at the things which are not seen. The things which are seen are temporary, but the things which are not seen are eternal.

> Trust in the Lord with all thine heart; and lean not to
> thine own understanding.
>
> In all thine ways acknowledge him and he shall direct
> your paths (Proverbs 3:5-6).

Our relationship with God brings us into the knowledge of his word and allows us access to his presence. The established relationship gives us the benefit to ask for anything according to His will and He assures us that we can have it.

Prayer Restores Broken Lives
And Heals Wounds

Sometimes we know our purpose, but because of fear, the pressure of public opinion, or even our own slothfulness, we allow ourselves to be deceived by the devil. A few years ago I went through some things, which wounded my spirit to the point where I decided to walk away from my calling. It wasn't that I didn't know better, but because of the pressure of other people's opinions I decided to throw in the towel and give up. I heard a minister say that you can't throw the towel in the ring and quit anytime you decide that you want to because God owns the ring and he sets the rules. The wonderful thing about God is that He never gives up on us even when we decide to give up. For whom the Lord loves he corrects; therefore we are not to despise the chastening of the Lord, neither be weary of his correction.

In our Christian walk, there are times God allows us to be broken or crushed. Believe me, I understand that the process of being broken and crushed is difficult to endure but it is necessary. The willingness to allow God to break shows we are willing to be reconstructed and refined. Once I heard a minister preaching at my home church and what he said made so much sense and encouraged me in the situation that I was going through. He said that *the olive does not yield olive oil until it has been crushed, neither do grapes give wine. To release the full potential of the olive and grape, each has to be placed under pressure.* To release our full potential, we have to be broken. The impurities of our heart and mind must be removed.

> The heart is deceitful above all things, and desperately wicked: who can know it? Jeremiah 17:9

> Likewise the Spirit also helpeth our infirmities: for we know not what we should pray for as we ought: but the Spirit itself maketh intercession for us with groanings which cannot be uttered.

> And he that searcheth the hearts knoweth what is the mind of the Spirit, because he maketh intercession for the saints according to the will of God (Romans 8:26-27).

In the holy scriptures, man is referred to as a vessel, a person into whom some quality is infused or simply a container. The vessels were made from raw clay, which is softened with water so it will be malleable. The lump of clay is thrown on wheel, pressed, pounded, at times cut into pieces, then, the shaped clay is placed in fire.

> Then I went down to the potter's house, and, behold, he wrought a work on the wheels.

And the vessel that he made of clay was marred in the hand of the potter: so he made it again another vessel, as seemed good to the potter to make it. (Sometimes when we mess up are fall short in life we have been marred all we have to do is repent and allow God to make us over again).

Then the word of the LORD came to me, saying,

O house of Israel, cannot I do with you as this potter? saith the LORD. Behold, as the clay is in the potter's hand, so are ye in mine hand, O house of Israel (Jeremiah 18: 3-6).

Until you have been crushed and placed under fire to be purified, you cannot fully reflect God's image.

In our process, God teaches us about himself. He shows us that there are different ways for him to manifest. We have a tendency to put the limitations on the way God moves or put Him in a particular pattern. If the spirit of God is demonstrated in a fashion that we are not familiar with, we are so quick to be judgmental. We must realize that God is not small and simple minded. He is not limited in His actions. He chose to use the foolish things of this world to confound the wise (I Corinthians 1:27). The problem is we do not always recognize him. It was the prophet Isaiah who looked for the Lord to speak to a very grandiose manner. However, the Lord did the opposite of what he *thought*.

And he said, Go forth, and stand upon the mount before the LORD. And, behold, the LORD passed

> by, and a great and strong wind rent the mountains,
> and brake in pieces the rocks before the LORD; but
> the LORD was not in the wind: and after the wind an
> earthquake; but the LORD was not in the earthquake:
>
> And after the earthquake a fire; but the LORD was not
> in the fire: and after the fire a still small voice (I Kings
> 19:11-12).

Should you find yourself in this dilemma, remember God will only operate through the law of his word.

From my personal experience, I found that God will speak to you in your time of testing. More than that, God will forewarn us of a test and provides the answer key, which is the Bible, to pass the challenge! Amazing! He allowed me to know that He had given me power to endure and overcome any task. Several months before a major storm hit my life the Lord forewarned me that it was coming and even confirmed it through another evangelist. Even being forewarned, in the midst of the test instead of letting His words strengthen me, and staying before Him in prayer, I submitted to my emotions and decided to quit. It doesn't matter how broken that you've become God knows how to take the brokenness and refine you into a vessel of honor (Jeremiah 18: 2-6). When you are walking in disobedience to the will of God for your life He will allow you to get in situations created by the enemy and use it to push you back in His presence.

> Behold I have created the smith that bloweth the coals
> in the fire and that bringeth forth an instrument for
> his work; and I have created the waster to destroy
> (Isaiah 54:16).

I tried to convince myself that things had gotten better. But actually from that point, my life began falling apart piece by piece. The final blow was the most devastating. After eighteen years of marriage, my husband and I separated.

In my spirit, I felt as if I had been ripped apart. I was hurt, confused, shocked, distraught, and any other adjective to describe my indescribable pain! I felt as though my life had come to an abrupt stop. A part of me just wanted to shut off from everyone and everything. I had known people, who went through separation from their spouses and witnessed how some became bitter. I didn't want to be like that because I felt it only made it harder on the children. Moreover, I didn't want to give Satan anymore leverage in our lives. I knew the only way I was going to make it through this was to return to God and prayer.

My first step was to repent. Even though I did not deserve forgiveness, God restored me. It took time but God healed me of the wound. All before I was content to be in the outer court, to simply feel the residue of his spirit. However, this time I knew that was not enough. At first, I was seeking Him to fix all the wrongs in my life. However, God intended for me to willingly let go of those desires and to seek intimacy with him. I began to have a new outlook on life, which is incredible! I have to admit, at first, I sought the presence of God out of sheer desperation. *God, I need to fix this or work this out for me.* However, my desperation turned into a pursuit of God's presence. Nothing else mattered. All I wanted was more and more of God. I discovered that it does not matter what you fill your life with you will not be satisfied until you have come to know God. There was an insatiable hunger in me that could only be filled by God.

I thank God for Tommy Tenny and the books on *God Chasers and the Prayers of a God Chaser*. Those books helped me to realize the very things I was running from, the pain and the brokenness, were the very things which helped to draw me into the presence of God. The most memorable example he used was the cry of your child when they are hurt and how you would respond to that cry. I had made up my mind that the devil wasn't going to get any glory out of what was happening in my life. I began praying and seeking God's face desperately. I needed to have the love and peace of him to fill the brokenness and heal the hurt in me. I asked him to fill me with his love in abundance so that I would not become bitter and full of anger and hatred. I needed God to fill me with his love that I would be able to love others as he does, unconditionally, regardless of their past or their wrongs. I continuously asked God to allow my life to be a reflection of him. I sought God with all of my being. I completely surrendered myself to him and allowed him to empty me of "myself", my will and my motives, and my view of life. As a result, my pursuit of Him became different.

When you began to cry out to God out of the depths of your soul with a pure heart, he will break down walls in your life, heal your broken spirit, and restore you. Now, I can look back on my experiences with praises in my soul because the weapon that the enemy formed to destroy me became the thing that brought me closer to God. After Joseph's brothers had faked his death, forced him into a pit, and sold him into slavery, he was able to rejoice in the end, as well.

> Now therefore be not grieved, nor angry with
> yourselves, that ye sold me hither: for God did send me
> before you to preserve life.

For these two years hath the famine been in the land:
and yet there are five years, in the which there shall
neither be earing nor harvest.

And God sent me before you to preserve you a
posterity in the earth, and to save your lives by a great
deliverance.

So now it was not you that sent me hither, but God:
and he hath made me a father to Pharaoh, and lord of
all his house, and a ruler throughout all the land of
Egypt (Genesis 45:5-8.

The hurt designed to pull us away from God becomes the
ammunition to push us to God. The hurt pushes us to pray and
seek the face of God.

As I began to stay before him in prayer, the things that seemed
to distract me no longer interested me. Friends, who I associated
with, removed themselves from my presence. On first thought, it
seems I would be upset but I was not bothered. I had me more
quality time to spend in the word of God. You will prioritize your
life. You will be able to see the need to place God first. Jesus said
to his disciples, "If any man come after me, let him deny himself,
and take up his cross and follow me" (Matthew 16:24). You have to
be willing to lay aside "you". Your personal agenda must give way
to the purpose and plan of God. Yes, we have ideas and dreams;
however, the ideas and dreams God has for us supersedes anything
we could ever possibly imagine. The manifestation of God in our
lives brings an immeasurable glory, which can only be given by
God (Romans 8:18; Philippians 3:4-10).

The Apostle Paul could have boasted concerning the things that he had achieved through his Jewish heritage and earlier religious training. Yet, he did not. Paul realized that none of these things could bring him to God.

> But what things were gain to me, those I counted loss
> for Christ.

> Yea doubtless, and I count all things but loss for
> the excellency of the knowledge of Christ Jesus my
> Lord: for whom I have suffered the loss of all things,
> and do count them but dung, that I may win Christ
> (Philippians 3:7-8)

We have to forget those things that are behind us and press toward the mark for the prize of the higher calling of God in Christ Jesus (Phil. 3:14). When you become hungry in your spirit because of your need to know him, and began to diligently seek after him compassionately with all your heart he will meet you at the point of your need. He is a rewarder of them that will diligently seek Him (Hebrews 11:6). To diligently seek him is to pursue him with all your heart and mind no matter what the cost. You will come to a point that your only desire will be to know him and please him. *Blessed are they which do hunger and thirst after righteousness: for they shall be filled* (Matthew 5:6). The uncontrollable craving produces a passionate pursuit for intimacy which is only satiated when God reveals himself to you. Yet, the craving and longing is so strong that you have to keep going back to God for more and more. *If any man thirst, let him come unto me and drink* (John 7:37). You will find the closer you get to God, the more distant you will be with everything else around you. Most of your time will be spent seeking time to be in his presence. In the presence of the Lord, we find joy, peace, and contentment. Remember this level of intimacy is going to cost you. You have to give up sin and the cares of the world (Hebrews 12:1). The price paid cannot be compared to the glory that will be revealed in you. The contentment you gain from his presence is beyond words.

God desires us to seek him out of love. If you're just seeking him for no other reason than you love him and want to know him intimately, he's waiting to reveal himself to you. *He said behold I stand at the door and knock. If anyone hears my voice and opens the door, I will come in to him and dine with him and he with Me (Revelation New King James Version. 3:20).* You have to be willing to be completely sold out to him. You have to be willing to die from your desires, so you can walk and live in his spirit.

For many of us, it is the "killing" of fleshly desires, which is one of our greatest battles. It is not going to be easy but it is a must. If Satan can hold you captive to your carnal desires, he will keep you a prisoner and you will not experience the freedom you can have in God. Remember the choice is always yours! Your flesh or emotions are the only part of you that he can touch to bring destruction. There is going to be a struggle simply because Satan does not give up and accept defeat. As Christians, we need to take on this mentality and refuse to accept defeat, knowing that through Christ we are more than conquers in Him and we have already been given victory. In order to receive the promises of God, we've got to fight with a vengeance and take the promises of God for our lives by force. Matt. 11:12, states that the kingdom of heaven suffereth violence and the violent take it by force. This means the enemy is going to come against believers in all forms trying to destroy them and discredit the work of God in our lives, home, family, church, community and in our ministries. We have to arm ourselves with the word of God, prayer, and fight with a vengeance storming the gates of hell and taking the things that rightfully belong to us as the people of God. Still, the power to do this comes from being in the presence of the Lord. You will find that there is nothing more rewarding than to walk in fellowship with God.

There are many Christians struggling with the temporal value system of this world such as the demons of religiosity, traditions, and positions. They are allowing themselves to lose out when it comes to knowing God and experiencing salvation or walking in the newness of life in Christ. If you haven't received salvation, which is newness of life through Christ Jesus, your statues in life, your church duties, are your church affiliations with denominations will not be enough to secure your eternal life with Christ. The enemy is deceiving so many people into being comfortable with the idea that as long as they join a church and work a position, they are alright. Then, there are others caught up in their family denominations and church affiliations that they don't even know the realness of Christ as in having him as their personal savior.

One day, my youngest daughter and I were riding together when we came upon a small community. The stretch of the community was no more two or three miles at the most. Within that little stretch, there were three churches sitting almost a quarter of a mile from each other. The community was so small that one church could have probably held all of the people. My daughter looked at me and said, "That's so sad". I responded, "What are you talking about?" She said, "As small as this place is, why are there three churches sitting right on each other, one was a Baptist, the other Apostolic, and the other Holiness? If we are all serving God and striving for the same purpose, why is it necessary to have so many churches in the same area?" I explained to her this was a prime example of the demon of religiosity or denominationalism that divides the body of Christ.

Anytime that you take a doctrine, denomination, tradition, or your title concerning the position that you are holding in the church and make it more important than the preaching of the gospel and winning souls for the kingdom, you are offering up strange fire before the lord. In a sense you are doing the same thing as Aaron's sons, and they paid severely with their own lives. Our first responsibility, as believers of the gospel, is to witness to the loss and win souls for the kingdom. I was really amazed to know that some people join the church and even hold certain positions in the local church because some of their jobs require it.

If you have not been born again and accepted Jesus Christ as your personal savior, your eternal life is unsecured and your soul is damned to Hell. When we have been redeemed by the blood of Jesus, we are to function as one body. We are to work in unity to make up the body of Christ and prepare ourselves to be the bride of Christ, awaiting his return to wrath us away.

Prayer Will Tear Down Strong holds And Bring Deliverance In Our Lives

Through prayer, we receive deliverance from strongholds, which are habits and hang ups that some were entangled with before we received salvation and even some that we are still not delivered from after being saved. The greatest stronghold that we need God to break is in our minds. First, we have to realize a stronghold is a spirit or spirits, which carry and produce other spirits which build a fortress in the mind. It is in this fortress the devil will inject negative thoughts of lust, pride, fear, doubt, and disbelief in us concerning the circumstances or situations in our lives. Our thoughts are like seeds. When given the right conditions, the seed will develop and produce fruit. Once a thought is planted, it will begin to grow and reproduce other thoughts of its kind. The devil uses those thoughts to dominate or control us in our minds and our flesh concerning the decisions we make.

For this reason we need to meditate on the word of God day and night. David wrote, "Thy word have I hid in mine heart, that I might not sin against thee" (Psalm 119:11). If we learn to trust and seek Him, He promises to keep our minds in perfect peace. Isaiah 26:3 says, "Thou wilt keep him in perfect peace whose mind is stayed on thee: because he trusted in thee". Despite the way God chooses to move, we have to trust God even when we don't understand His plans. Isaiah 26:12 declares that Lord would ordain peace for us. The more you seek Him and fill yourself with His word those ways and habits that are not of Christ you will find yourself letting go of because your desires have changed and there's no room for them.

Let's say you have a container of milk and you add water to the milk. The milk becomes diluted. The more water you add will displace the milk. Therefore, the carton will be filled with water has the milk empties out. Instead of having milk, you will have water. The same thing occurs with the word of God. The more you pray and fill your spirit on the word of God everything else is in you is going to be "emptied out". The only substance left in you will be the spirit of God. There will be no room for anything else. The word of God has the power to deliver you and set you free if you will allow it to. As you continue to pray and read the word, your spirit will become filled. He will strengthen you and transform your inner man to the point that you will reflect Him outwardly.

As you pray and stay in the presence of God, He will not only transform you, but He will turn you into a transformer. During your conversations with those around you, the word that is in you will transform them. John 7:38, states "He that believeth on me as the scripture hath said, out of his belly shall flow rivers of living water". The word of God and the anointing of God inside of you is the living water that will come out of your belly and the word will become life to all of those who receive it. "For I will pour water upon them that is thirsty, and floods upon the dry grounds" (Isaiah 44:3).

The mind is very powerful. The mind controls and sets the pattern for the rest of the body. The person, who is a hypochondriac, constantly seeks medical attention for imaginary physical ailments created in their mind. These imaginary aliments are so extreme the individual believes they are in massive pain. This example lends itself as evidence that the mind is able influence the body to project its will.

After we are saved it is necessary for us to have a renewing of the mind by taking on the mind of Christ. Proverb 4:23 states "it's important to guard our hearts and minds and be careful of what we allow them to be filled with because out of it springs the issues of life (Proverbs 4:23, and Phil.4:7). Through prayer, God gives us a peace that passes all understanding and will keep our hearts and minds. Today's Christians do not guard their minds carefully enough. We fill our minds with television programs, radio, the Internet, newspapers, magazines, novels, movies, and worldly conversations. Even though some of those things have a positive influence, we also have to stop and see the negative effects of them. From each of those, we form thoughts in our minds. Therefore, when we see and listen to negative things that are full of corruption, these thoughts cater to the desires of the flesh, and we are contaminating our spirit. We have to realize that the eyes are the windows or gates to our souls. That is why David said in Psalms 101:3, "I will set nothing wicked before my eyes". The eyes are vitally important because they are passage ways or entrances. They are reflectors that send pictures and signals to the mind, which allows the mind to form thought patterns. Our mind is like a computer. Once we look on something, it has been stored in our memory.

The first time "seeing" was mentioned in the Bible, in its proper context, was in Genesis. "And God saw," meaning that God saw His reflection in the thing that He had created and He said that it was good. We have to realize that before God created anything it was a thought. It began in His mind. Before man's eyes were opened to sin, he saw everything as God. Man saw the created world as God did, in purity and perfection. All of creation a harmonious organism, working together in obedience and unity being subjected to man's authority as man was reflecting God, which was good. After the sin of disobedience, man's eyes were opened in the natural. Man saw knowledge and understanding in the wrong direction. This means man had become sensitive and alive to sin. In this, he became sensitive to the natural, carnal, and the satanic leaving him spiritually blind or blind to the divine.

Consequently, through the eyes is where Satan first invaded humanity and brought destruction in the three God given areas of human life, which were the emotional, the physical, and the spiritual. He planted a spirit of rebellion which caused disobedience, "and the woman *saw that the tree was good for food* (Genesis 3:6,7). He planted a thought or a mental picture which invaded the emotions stimulating the lust of the flesh and it was pleasant for the eyes. The lusting of the eyes caused sin to take affect in the physical. It arouses pride, promotes selfishness, and increases a drive for power to exalt oneself, which affects the spiritual part of man, in turn, causing man to become rebellious and disobedient which led to the fall.

Jesus characterized as being the second Adam, conceived of the spirit, and born of flesh had to endure the same temptations. Satan tried to defeat Him in the same three areas; however, Satan used a different technique. By using the power of the word of God, Jesus showed us one of our strongest defenses against a satanic attack. After fasting for forty days, Satan knew that Jesus was hungry. Trying to use the weakness of the flesh, Satan challenged Jesus' identity in an effort to cause him to sin out of anger. The emotional state of Jesus was tested.

> And when the tempter came to him, he said, If thou be the Son of God, command that these stones be made bread.

> But he answered and said, It is written, Man shall not live by bread alone, but by every word that proceedeth out of the mouth of God (Matthew 4:3-4).

Seeing that He could not attack Jesus through his emotions, Satan, again, challenges Jesus in the physical by showing him all the kingdoms of the world and promising their glory to him, if Jesus would fall down and worship him. The riches of the world are vast and pleasant to the eyes. This test represented the lust of eyes. Yet, again, Jesus responded with the word of God.

> Then saith Jesus unto him, Get thee hence, Satan: for it is written, Thou shalt worship the Lord thy God, and him only shalt thou serve (Matthew 4:10).

There are times when Satan will present things to us with a promise. Being gullible and looking at the "thing" with natural eyes instead of having a spiritual insight, we open ourselves up to deception. When he promised all the kingdoms of the world to Jesus, Satan could not have given them to Him. The kingdoms of the world belong to Jesus, who was God made manifest in the flesh as the ultimate sacrifice(Psalm 22:27-28). Satan paints a beautiful picture to us concerning things we desire. My friends do not be deceived by him. Satan never gives you anything without extreme consequence.

Satan's unwillingness to accept defeat brings, yet, another challenge to Jesus. The scripture states Satan took Jesus up into the holy city, sets him on the pinnacle of the temple, and says to Him, "If you be the Son of God throw yourself down. For it is written that He shall give His angels charge over you, and in their hands they shall bear you up lest you dash your foot against a stone" (Matthew 4:5-6 New King James Version). The challenge here was with the pride of life. Jesus answered, "It is written again, you shall not tempt the Lord your God" (Matthew 4:7 New King James Version). This lets us know that when we really trust God we don't have to put Him to a test or try to prove him to anyone.

It is sad to say but some Christians today are arrogant, full of pride, and glory seekers. They find themselves trying to prove God to people. This is really unnecessary. God can prove Himself at any time; therefore, God does not want us to put on some form of entertainment. Whenever the opportunity to witness and pray with someone arises, the only thing we are required to do is speak God's word. We are to say only what he says and do what he has instructed us to do in the situation. Most of all, in our everyday living, we are to lift Him up by walking in the beauty of holiness. Through holy living, God is truly reflected in us. He said that if we would lift Him up from the earth that He would draw all men unto Himself. All that He requires of us is to let the light of Him shine through.

Strongholds are manifested both naturally and spiritually. Therefore, we have to constantly pray to God asking him to keep us humble. The pride of life is a stronghold that is easily entertained if we are not watchful. Whenever the spirit of God has used us in an awesome manner, if we are not careful, people will sometimes cause us to except credit that we are not due. Satan tried this with Jesus: *if you be the Son of God.* Because Jesus knew who he was and knew his divine purpose, He didn't try to prove himself to Satan. We should know who we are in Christ and know the purpose in our lives and never try convince anyone of who we are, or of the anointing that is working in us. Psalms 139:23 states that we need to continuously ask God to search us, and know our hearts, try us, and know our thoughts. Daily we must ask God to let the words of our mouth and the meditation of our hearts be acceptable in His sight (Psalms 19:14). We must pray that God will create in us a clean heart and renew His spirit in us daily as not to fall prey to Satan's tactics (Psalms 51:10).

When we are bound by strongholds, there are times when it takes us persevering in prayer along with fasting to be released. We may even need to have others pray with us in an agreement prayer. Matthew 18:19-20 demonstrates the power of agreement in prayer. The agreement prayer is a powerful because you have joined forces on earth and brought the forces of heaven in the midst of the situation (Matthew 18:19-20). In this instance, Jesus puts himself and the Father at our command in the midst of the petition. He said that "whatever you've asked shall be done of His father which is in heaven". Only God can make such a binding covenant. Only God can fulfill such a promise and reach its exact and all-controlling demands.

For instance, with some addictions such as smoking, of which I can relate because that was my crutch, there are occasions when a person doesn't really crave for cigarettes in their body, but within their minds. Sometimes, even as a person smokes, they think within their mind *I really don't want to smoke,* but the fear of not having a cigarette to smoke brings on a need to have it. Here fear and craving have joined forces to create a mental stronghold. The compulsion to smoke is so strong; it literally holds you and you conform to the unction. At this point, you are under the influence of the lust of the eye and you allow yourself to be seduced by the craving of nicotine. Still, there are habits you want to be free from, but, your body craves. After going without something you are addicted to for a while, the body will start to react. Regardless to what it is, through prayer, God can and will break the chains over your life if you ask and allow him. God will deliver you from any habit no matter the length of time you have been addicted.

Also, he will free you from the fear that binds you to it. Fear works with evil just as faith works with righteousness. Faith produces freedom; yet, fear binds you. For God has not given us the spirit of fear, but of power, and of love and of a sound mind (II Timothy 1:7). I John 4:18 supports that fact that perfect love casts out fear, because fear involves torment. Once you have allowed the perfect love of God to take complete control of your life, you'll find that the only thing that you need to be content is Jesus.

The Necessitie Of Praying For Wisdom And Knowledge

In order to obtain wisdom, we must become disciplined in our spirit and in our walk with Christ which comes through prayer. Wisdom is the skill for living that comes from instructions and understanding. It is the divine and spiritual treasure that rests in the hands of God, since it comes from above, it is impossible to attain it apart from Him. The fear of the Lord is the beginning of wisdom (Proverbs 9:10). This fear means reverence, having respect for God, and the things of God.

For the Lord gives wisdom; from His mouth comes knowledge and understanding (Proverbs 2:6). As we seek Him in prayer, He gives us wisdom, the ability to use the best means, at the best time, to accomplish the best results in every situation. Our ability to trust God is directly the result of our knowledge of God. The better we know Him the more we can trust him. The only way that we can get to know Him is through His word and in prayer. As we talk to Him in prayer and listen to His voice through the scriptures, we become intimate with Him. True wisdom is being able to see life from God's perspective. If you were raised with Christ seek those things which are above, where Christ is sitting on the right hand of God (Colossians 3:1-3). Set your mind on things above, not on things on the earth. Our minds should be focused on seeking the righteousness of God that you can allow the kingdom of God to be manifested in you here on earth. Don't set your minds on earthly material things because in time they will perish. Be concerned about the things of God and fulfilling your destiny in Him seeking His will for your life. I am not saying that we are not to ask Him to bless us with material things, but don't allow your seeking Him for the blessings of material things take precedence over your desire to please Him and know Him intimately. Begin to seek him and appreciate him because he is not only God in your life, but, let him become the God of your life. For ye are dead, and your life is hid with Christ in God (Colossians 3:3). As we pray, God will give us the wisdom to live a life of beauty, fulfillment, and purpose, under the dominion of God (Proverbs 3:15-18). James 1:5 states "if any man lacks wisdom, let him ask of God who gives to all men liberally and without reproach, and it will be given to him". God will give us the wisdom and knowledge to pray when we are confronted with adverse situations. He will allow us to know how to obtain victory in the midst of any storm arises in our lives.

God Responds To Prayers From The Heart

Our prayers are only effective when we pray from our hearts in faith. Heart felt prayers are filled with fervor. In order for the petition to move God, it must first move you. When you become passionate about a petition to the point that you are moved by it, then you will give it your best. There is a difference between a regular prayer and a passionate prayer. A prayer of passion comes through brokenness. It is the passion concerning the situation that will pull God into your presence because He loves the smell of passion. When you are passionate, your soul is bowed down and your spirit is broken before the Lord. Psalms 51: 17 says that the sacrifices of God are a "broken spirit, a broken and contrite heart, these O God, You will not despise". He is touched with the feelings of our infirmities; therefore, the residue from passionate prayers lingers before the heart of God. When passion along with faith touches God, He is moved to respond to our petitions. For instance, the woman with the issue of blood touched Jesus and was made whole immediately. The woman never touched His body physically, but the intensity of her faith, the passion of her belief, her overwhelming need, surpassed the all the others in the crowed.

Having faith in God is the main ingredient in ones ability to pray effectively; therefore, I would consider faith as our foundation. Prayer is simply faith resting in, acting with, leaning on, and obeying God. In order to activate our faith, there has to be a work. Without a work, faith is dead. You must believe that God hears your prayers and in His ability to answer them. I consider prayer to be faith at work. It is absolutely necessary for a person to have faith in order to receive salvation, for with the heart one believes unto righteousness, and with the mouth confession is made unto salvation (Romans 10:10). Hebrew 11:1 states "now faith is the substance of things hoped for, the evidence of things not seen".

I believe faith is a God inspired attribute that was instilled in man's since his creation. This is the part man that allows him to believe and acknowledge that all creation is being sustained by a supreme, sovereign power. Faith is having the ability to trust God completely in every situation regardless to what it is or how it looks. It's being able to call those things that are not as though they were, because you're not seeing the situation through the natural eyes but with spiritual insight. Faith is having confidence in God's word that we will perform. Hebrews 11:6 tells us that without faith it is impossible to please Him. He who comes to God must believe that He is and that He is a rewarder of those who diligently seek Him. The believers of Jesus Christ should live by faith. When we pray we must believe God's word even though there is nothing visible to touch or see.

Faith is the greatest unused power in the universe. It has no limitations and knows no boundaries except the ones that we allow to be set through our little finite minds. When we seek God in prayer, we don't have to fix our words to make it sound good. Our prayers need only to come from the depths of our souls. We cry out to God, desiring to know him. Our praise and adoration, along with the compassion and sincerity in what we are saying, is what draws his attention to us.

Whenever you find yourself having a difficult time finding the words to say, those are the times you began to worship Him and give Him thanks. As you stay before God asking Him to teach you to pray, he will do it. The Holy Spirit within you will take over and make intercession in your behalf. God knows you intimately and loves you unconditionally. He knows your desires even when you don't know exactly how to express yourself. God loved you so that He gave the very best of himself to save you from your sins in order that you would be able to live a life of abundance without condemnation. God is touched by a heart of compassion as it comes before Him desiring to know Him. When our prayers touch God's heart, he is moved to respond.

When We Turn Our Souls To God Our Humanity Takes On His Divinity Transforming Us Into His Image

Prayer is a place where humanity and divinity come together. After we have accepted God in our lives, the Holy Spirit that is in us prays through us making intercessions to the father in our behalf. The more we pray in the spirit we are allowing Jesus to transform us into his image. We're pulling off the old nature of sin, which was passed to us from Adam. During this process, we are being reborn and transformed in our souls by the spirit and through the blood of Jesus Christ. Prayer is the turning of the human soul to the living God (Psalms 25:1-22). In John 17:10, 22, Christ prayed for His disciples and even for all the believers. He was making the request that our humanity would take on His divinity through salvation and that we would become one with Him in the spirit. He says, "And all mine are yours, and yours are mine, and I am glorified in them. And the glory which you gave me, I have given them, that they maybe one just as we are one."

In the Old testament, man lived under the law; consequently, the spirit of God came upon man (Judges 3:10 and Judges 13:25).

The law was to instruct the people about the person and ways of their redeemer so that they could be set apart to a life of holiness and obedience. It was not to save anyone but to reveal the people's need to trust in the Lord. Now, with the new covenant, which is through Jesus Christ, the spirit of the Lord dwells in man.

> For He has made the two one and has destroyed the barrier, the dividing wall of hostility by abolishing in His flesh the law with its commandments and regulations (Ex. 34:33-35, IICor. 3:13-18).

Under the law when Moses had been in the presence of God, he had to put a veil over his face, so that the children of Israel could not look steadily at his face, because of the glory of his continence. Now, in prayer through the New Covenant, which is Christ, we can go into the presence of God with unveiled faces beholding as a mirror, the glory of the Lord. For through Jesus, we have access to the Father by one spirit (Galatians 3:23-27). Before faith came, we were kept guarded by the laws of Moses and the law was our tutor to bring us to Christ. After faith came, we were no longer under a tutor, for we are all sons of God through Jesus Christ. We are baptized in Christ through the Holy Spirit and have put on Christ. As we go before Him in repentance and faith, we are being gloriously transformed more and more fully through His word, into His image by the Holy Spirit. After Jesus defeated Satan on Calvary, he paid the penalty of death for our sins and brought us back in to the presence of God. We all became as priests. This gave us the ability to put on divinity and go boldly before the throne of God.

> But you are a chosen generation, a royal priesthood,
> a holy nation, His own special people that you may
> proclaim the praises of Him who called you out of
> darkness into the marvelous light (I Peter 2:9).

Prayer is the greatest untapped resource available to us. It's untapped eternal power that is invincible and impossible to defeat. As we stay before the Lord in prayer, His spirit should be evident in us. The presence of the Spirit of Christ is what moves upon the hearts of those to whom we witness. When we are completely sold out for the cause of Christ, our lives should become living epistles, like the lives of the apostles in the scriptures.

> But you shall receive power when the Holy Spirit has
> come upon you; and you shall be witness to me (Acts
> 1:8).

When we really learn who we are in Christ and discover our purpose, we will be able to rise above any circumstance and rejoice in the midst of persecution. We have to learn the secret of developing an eternal perspective in the midst of earthly problems as Peter, John, Paul, and the other Apostles did in the past. They knew who they were in Christ and believed on his word. They were willing to transform their world at any price, even at the cost of their lives. When we read about their ministry and how awesome the anointing flowed through them to work miracles and wonders. For some unknown reason, we seem to think that this happened because they were extraordinary people.

I would like to assure you that they were not. They were devout men who completely gave themselves over to prayer and fasting. They did not see the scriptures as *word on a page of parchment.*

They viewed the word of God as the means to change the world. By walking in the Spirit of Christ, they were able to prove the word by doing "greater" works. The word assures us that God is no respecter of persons. Total surrender and submission to God to be used for His glory, He will do the same thing in us. Now that we are saved we, too, have become disciples; therefore, we should be working the works of Christ with the same effects as the apostles and doing even greater works. We have the freedom to do so without having anyone take our lives for making mention of the name of Jesus.

As we read about all the miracles, signs, and wonders that Jesus performed when He was here on earth, most of us think he did this because He was God's son or even to prove to the world that he was God's Son. This was not the case. Because Jesus knew who He was and understood purpose, He had to demonstrate to us the eternal power that was given to Adam in the beginning and let us know the authority that He had given back to us while restoring back to the Father. From the beginning, all power had been given to Adam to have complete authority in earth. All that Christ did was to show us the authority we have if we live life God style. Jesus Christ showed us that we have everything subject to us or under our feet. While here on earth in the flesh, Jesus was a regular human being just like you and me. He understood His place of power. Through the power of prayer, we are even able to reach into the supernatural and access the things there that are available for us. This is were we have an abundance of resources such as healing, miracles, and many other faith gifts, and even natural things that we need for our daily provisions.

Prayer Gives Us Power To Speak God's Word With Boldness

As we pray, the Holy Spirit will give us the power to speak the word of God with boldness. Through prayer, we become sold out for the gospel of Christ as the apostles of old. Regardless of the persecution, they endured for the sake of the gospel of Jesus Christ. Even at the price of their own lives, they were willing to win souls for Christ. After the Sanhedrin commanded Peter and John not to preach or make mention of the name of Jesus, these men of God did not waiver. They continued to speak and teach in the name of Jesus. They would not allow the threats to stop them. During their personal prayer time, they even prayed God would grant them boldness.

> And when they prayed, the place where they had
> assembled together was shaken, and they were all filled
> with the Holy Spirit, and they spoke the word of God
> with boldness (Acts 4:31).

As believers of the gospel, we should be walking in the same authority today as they did. The same Jesus, who saved and delivered them, gave them power to speak His word with boldness and access heaven until things supernaturally happen for them. He is willing and waiting to do the same works in us today.

> Verily, Verily, I say unto you, He that believeth on me,
> the works that I shall do he shall do also; and greater
> works than these shall he do; because I go unto my
> father (John 14: 12-13).

Jesus tells us that whatever we ask in his name that He will do so that the Father maybe glorified in the Son. Now, is the time for us to bombard heaven with prayer to unlock the transforming power of Jesus Christ. It is time for us to walk in this level of spiritual authority so we will be able to turn the world upside down just as the apostles.

The main reason that we are not walking in this authority is because of the lack of prayer. Most of the saints either have a poor prayer life or no prayer life. Everybody is too caught up in the fast lane doing too many temporal things and not sacrificing the time that is needed to labor in prayer. I realize that there have been and still are now, some Apostles and Evangelists who are turning the world upside down and making an impressive mark on the lives of people for the sake of Christ. Yet, this does not mean that the rest of us are supposed get comfortable, be relaxed, and think that this is a work for them only because the harvest is great and the labors are still few. Jesus' mission was to save the lost harvest. The harvest refers to those who do not know Jesus as the savior.

> Luke 10:2
> Therefore said he unto them, The harvest truly is great,
> but the labourers are few: pray ye therefore the Lord of

the harvest, that he would send forth labourers into his harvest (Luke 10:2).

Matt. 18: 11-12

For the Son of man is come to save that which was lost.

How think ye? if a man have an hundred sheep, and one of them be gone astray, doth he not leave the ninety and nine, and goeth into the mountains, and seeketh that which is gone astray?

Luke 19:9-11

And Jesus said unto him, This day is salvation come to this house, forsomuch as he also is a son of Abraham.

For the Son of man is come to seek and to save that which was lost

The lack of prayer has caused us to become desensitized. Many Christians are devoid of spiritual sensitivity. Some Christians are operating off of a spiritual high, which soon fades. In the end, they loss faith and walk away from God. While others, seek to live off of the anointing of one who is prayerful and full of God's spirit. In the area I live, we call them the spiritual leeches. They try to attach to a strong believer to sap them of their anointing and spiritual strength. If the individual does not soon recognize this form of attack, the individual finds they are weak. Should the spiritual leech succeed in this form of satanic attack, they will soon *kill or severely wound* their host. From this point, the spiritual leech will look for another victim. Jesus warns us concerning spiritual attacks of this sort. In the parable of the five wise and five foolish virgins, Jesus is referring the condition of the church. There will be those who will be filled with the Spirit of God and are prayerfully awaiting his return. However, there will be those who will allow themselves to be caught unprepared.

> And the foolish said unto the wise, Give us of your oil; for our lamps are gone out.

> But the wise answered, saying, Not so; lest there be not enough for us and you: but go ye rather to them that sell, and buy for yourselves.

> And while they went to buy, the bridegroom came; and they that were ready went in with him to the marriage: and the door was shut (Matthew 25:8-10).

It is time to stop being thrill seekers and fall on our faces before God so that we may become laborers in the gospel. There is a whole world waiting to be feed and even the few dedicated men and women of God that are doing all they can still is not enough.

> 2 Corinthians 4:3 (Amplified Bible)
> But even if our Gospel (the glad tidings) also be hidden (obscured and covered up with a veil that hinders the knowledge of God), it is hidden [only] to those who are perishing and obscured [only] to those who are spiritually dying and veiled [only] to those who are lost.

So many Christians are running from revival to revival to see and hear the speaker of the hour. Most of them really do love the Lord as long as they can feel His spirit or be ushered into His presence through someone else's anointing. The problem is they do not want to commit themselves by sacrificing in prayer, fasting to kill their fleshly desires, and bring disciplined to do an effective work for Christ. After the revival is over, they can not live victoriously. True victory can only come through commitment. As Christians, we have to commit ourselves to God. It is our faith in the sure power of God, which evokes bold speech. To speak the word of God with boldness under the power and authority of the Holy Spirit, brings change in the lives of others. We, as Christians, need to become helpers in war to win souls for Christ. Jesus wants to use you to help reap the harvest of souls for the kingdom of God.

> And Jesus, walking by the sea of Galilee, saw two brethren, Simon called Peter, and Andrew his brother, casting a net into the sea: for they were fishers.
>
> And he saith unto them, Follow me, and I will make you fishers of men (Matthew 4:18-19)

My dad would say it this way, "no cross, no crown"! If we do not take up the fight to win souls for God's kingdom, we will not receive a crown. In order to reign with Him, we have to suffer with Him. The suffering we must endure does not compare to the glory of God that is revealed in us. During most difficult test or storm of life, the Apostle Paul encourages us it is a "light affliction".

> For our light affliction, which is but for a moment,
> worketh for us a far more exceeding and eternal weight
> of glory (II Corinthians 4:17)

For most of us when we use the phrase, *"power to speak the word of God with boldness"*, we think it only means power to witness and preach the gospel. Your assumption is correct. However, the phrase refers to the power to speak the word of God in your own life concerning your destiny, or in the midst of the situation that you may be going through.

Once you have repented and asked for forgiveness of your sins, God does not remember your past. Instead, He is forever reaching to establish your present. From your present, He can take you into your future, which is to walk in your divine destiny prepared by Him especially designed for you. When you find yourself in warfare with the adversary, your most powerful weapon is the word of God. The word is the only thing that was used to identify God, as himself. The word of God is infallible because it is God.

> In the beginning was the word, and the word was with
> God, and the word was God (John 1:1).

Therefore, when the Word of God is spoken in the authority of the Spirit of God, God moves.

> … for I am alert and active, watching over My word to
> perform it.
> (Jeremiah 1:12 Amplified Bible)

There are other statements used to describe His attributes and His character, such as holy, the Light, the bread of life, the good shepherd, and the door. Yet, these phrases do not prove his identity. The only term that confirms his identity is *the Word.*

> And the Word was made flesh, and dwelt among us,
> (and we beheld his glory, the glory as of the only
> begotten of the Father,) full of grace and truth (John
> 1:14).

When Jesus was led by the spirit into the wilderness to be tempted by the devil, the only weapon that he used to defeat Satan was the word of God. Jesus demonstrated the authority of God's word.

> For the word of God is quick and powerful, sharper
> than any two-edged sword (Hebrews 4:12).

In this spiritual war, Ephesians 6: 17 tells us that the word of God is our sword. Having been cleaned through the Word (John 15:3), we have legal right to use the Word of God like Jesus. We have the same power within us. Still, to operate on this level, we have to be spiritually mature. Growth comes through prayer. In the Bible, trees are symbolic of men.

> Blessed is the man that walketh not in the counsel of
> the ungodly, nor standeth in the way of sinners, nor
> sitteth in the seat of the scornful.

> But his delight is in the law of the LORD; and in his
> law doth he meditate day and night.

> And he shall be like a tree planted by the rivers of
> water, that bringeth forth his fruit in his season; his

leaf also shall not wither; and whatsoever he doeth
shall prosper (Psalm 1:1-3).

Trees have to be pruned. The cutting away of dead leaves, stems, and branches allows the tree to bring forth more fruit. As we grow spiritually, God separates us from ungodliness by pruning us. He cuts way everything that is dead weight and unproductive.

Every branch in me that beareth not fruit he taketh
away: and every branch that beareth fruit, he purgeth
it, that it may bring forth more fruit (John 15:2).

LEARNING TO WALK IN THE AUTHORITY OF THE WORD

Using prayer, in its deepest sincerity, there is no force that can prevail against it. As we read in Acts 16: 25-26, even as Paul and Silas were praying and singing hymns to God, from a Philippian prison, God delivered them through a miraculous display of power. Suddenly, there was a great earth quake, so that the foundations were shaken, and immediately all the doors were open and everyone in chains were loosed (Acts 16:26). The same power is still available today for all who will seek God's will for their lives and trust him. When we are under attack by spirits of fear, depression, addictions, sickness, and disease, they desire to imprison us. However, effective and fervent prayer forces these demonic jailers to release us from their prisons.

In every day, the cares of life act like a type of tormenting prison. The prison tries to lock us down with poverty, threats of terrorism, among the dilemmas of famine and natural disaster. Nevertheless, God gives us a pattern to mark. Sincere prayer, coupled with praise and worship, will shake the foundation or the walls of these things to the point that we will be released. In addition, those around us will be freed as well. Acts 16:26 stated that all the doors were opened, and every one's bands were loosed! Your fervent prayers can unleash a manifestation of God's power. Everyone connected to you will go free. Whether or not these people want to be freed, they were set free by the mighty move of God's spirit.

> Not by might, nor by power, but by my spirit, saith the LORD of hosts (Zechariah 4:6)

> Now unto him that is able to do exceeding abundantly above all that we ask or think, according to the power that worketh in us
> (Ephesians 3:20)

In a sense, this is an untapped power God is waiting for us to open. In my mind's eye, I can see a wall being pushed by the force of water it tries hold back. If more pressure is added, the wall will crumble giving way to a continuing flow. The more pressure we added through prayer, the door to this level of anointing will be forced open and the flow of presence of God will be constant and continual.

There have been some occasions where I had to speak God's word in situations. As I spoke his word, he miraculously performed and met every need. I can recall the day my second oldest daughter was in a terrible accident at the age of nine. It was on her eighth birthday that she accepted Christ in her life as her personal savior. My daughter Regina was riding with my stepsister. They were taking her car in to be serviced on December 23rd. The driver of the other car fell asleep on the way home after working the midnight shift. Although the crash was a head on collision, most of the impact was on my daughter's side of the car. When the rescue squad reached them, they had to cut the car to remove my daughter. By the time

I left work and reached the local hospital, I was informed she had to be transported to another hospital. The local hospital was not equipped to care for her sustained injuries. She was transported to a hospital in Wilmington, North Carolina. By this time, news had traveled to my pastor, family, and friends. They were all praying for my daughter. When I reached the hospital in Wilmington, the doctors were busy working. Finally, one of her doctors came to explain the severity of her situation and that he would periodically give me updates on her situation. In each of his updates, he would tell me that they were finding more and more internal damage; while at the same time telling what they were doing to help my child. I told the doctor to do what he must but I would pray. Because I knew God worked in the power of agreement, I would call home and inform my pastor of Regina's condition. Knowing that there is strength in agreement, my pastor would update the saints that were making intercessions on my daughter's behalf.

The doctors came to me with several different reports. They would say they thought they were going to have to do surgery on her but changed their minds because there was no need. Whatever problems they discovered in the beginning, they would recheck her and find nothing. Finally, one of doctor explained to me that there must have been something wrong with the machine. I was told that they had taken two x-rays before the surgeon came and they didn't see the need for surgery. I knew that there was nothing wrong with their machine. With every update, my family members and I would God on her behalf. God was miraculously making the repairs in her body. She was in a comma, for which she stayed for approximately ten days, and her pelvic bone was broken. The Sunday following the accident, my pastor ministered to me during morning worship service. Under the leading of the Holy Spirit, she instructed me to place my head down at my daughter's ear and speak life to her.

On that day, I returned to the hospital in the critical care unit I sat down beside her bed. I leaned over to her ear and using the authority of the name of Jesus I began to speak life into her body. I began to command that every organ in her body to function normally and that she be made whole. I reminded God of his word that healing was the children's bread and He said that the power of life and death was in the tongue. I reminded him that He said with His stripes we were already healed and I was accepting that healing on my daughter's behalf. I was using the power of the word to speak life back in to her body. Before I left the hospital as I talked to her, I asked her to wiggle her fingers or grip my hand if she could hear me and she responded. I was grateful to God for that but I still believed him for a complete turn around. Prior to leaving, the medical staff told me they needed to move her from the critical care unit to the intensive care unit. However, I could not stay. I had to leave and take my other two daughters back home that night. In the same night, Regina regained consciousness. All of the machines were taken off of her and she was put into a regular room.

Although her pelvic bone was fractured and her legs in traction in order to keep her hips level, in less than a week, the attending doctor ordered her legs and hips out of traction because she asked them to. Several days later, Regina decided she did not want to ride in the wheel chair anymore, so they gave her a walker. When the attending doctor came by for her check up, he was upset that she was up walking around. He told the nurses that she should have been in a lot of pain. He thought I was pushing her to move too fast. Yet, he had authorized the chair and later the walker she had requested. One nurse explained to me that she told him when

Regina decided that she was able to walk I wasn't even there. I'd left to go home for a change and to check on my other children. He told me the next day that it was impossible for her to be up walking around without any pain. But, I knew that what seems impossible to man is possible with God. You see, where man's extremities end that is God's opportunity to do the exceptional. He asked the nurses if she had she been complaining about any pain. They told him that she had not. He wanted to keep her for two more days to see if she would ask for any pain medication. Because she did not he had to release her. Based on what the doctors noted and the accident report, Regina should have been in the hospital for months, but because of the power of fervent prayers she was home and about in less than a month's time.

> James 5:16 Amplified Bible
> The earnest (heartfelt, continued) prayer of a righteous
> man makes tremendous power available [dynamic in
> its working].

When we pray sincerely speaking God's words back to him concerning any situation in our lives His words will produce positive results.

BE PERISTENT IN YOUR PRAYERS AND REFUSE TO EXCEPT DEFEAT

Because all of us are different and come from various backgrounds, we have faced varying obstacles. Some are dealing with the bonds of drug abuse, physical abuse, prostitution, homosexuality, molestation, or even rape to name a few. Once you become a believer of Jesus Christ, the devil will try to make you *think* you can not be totally free of your past indiscretions or traumas. Satan uses the guilt of your past to trap you into believing you can't be better. However, God believes the opposite! The same God, who delivered over six million people out of slavery and worked miraculously to provide for them, is able to deliver you out of your bondage. Regardless of your sin, do not allow Satan to deceive you. There is a way out! God has never lost his power and He loves us unconditionally. God does not judge us, as man does. Man looks on the outside, but God judges the heart. No matter what you've done, or how bad you have been when you cry to God out of the depths of your soul with a true repentance heart, He will save you, deliver you, forgive you, and restore you. It only takes a few moments to repent but transformation takes time! Transformation is the process of becoming like God. To become like him, you must be persistent in prayer and dedicated to fasting. These techniques will breakdown the *old* you to allow the godly you shine through.

> II Corinthians 2:17
> Therefore if any man be in Christ, he is a new creature: old things are passed away; behold, all things are become new.

What is fasting? Fasting means to abstain from food or some other important necessity in order to give that time to God in prayer. We have to realize that God heard our prayers and probably has already released our answers, but sometimes hindering spirits on assignment from Satan are holding it up. Still, there are times when God doesn't release the answer immediately because He's desires us to learn patience or perhaps He is moving in another area of our lives which does not need to be revealed to us as yet. We are so quick to give up when things don't work out in our time frame. For many of us, this is where we lose. We forget that time is God's and he moves according to his will. To God, everything has a season, *a time*, and a purpose. Moving ahead of schedule or moving behind schedule is not a characteristic of God. His timing is precise and perfect.

> … being predestinated according to the purpose of him who worketh all things after the counsel of his own will
> (Ephesians 1:11).

> James 1: 3 & 4 Amplified Bible
> Be assured and understand that the trial and proving

of your faith bring out endurance and steadfastness
and patience.

But let endurance and steadfastness and patience have
full play and do a thorough work, so that you may
be [people] perfectly and fully developed [with no
defects], lacking in nothing.

An impatient attitude leads to rash decision making, which
opens the door for Satan to work. This is a very effective tool when
used by the devil. For Satan to have caused such chaos in heaven,
which led to his fall, he had to be a strategist.

Isaiah 14: 12-14
How art thou fallen from heaven, O Lucifer, son of the
morning! how art thou cut down to the ground, which
didst weaken the nations!

For thou hast said in thine heart, I will ascend into
heaven, I will exalt my throne above the stars of God: I
will sit also upon the mount of the congregation, in the
sides of the north:

I will ascend above the heights of the clouds; I will be
like the most High.

Unlike many of us, Satan does not except defeat. We know that
he is defeated and the God has is all powerful; yet, Satan still tries.
The reason many of us do receive our request is because we lack the
will to be persistent. Examine the scriptures from Isaiah 14: 12-
14. Isaiah shows us the attitude of Lucifer. His belief was *I will.*

His statements were personal commands he used to attempt his to overthrow God. Lucifer believed in his heart that he was able to carry out his mission. Although his plan failed, he believed.

> For as he thinketh in his heart, so is he ... (Proverbs 23:7).

It is time we change our mentality. As a Christians, we have to know we are more than conquers through Christ. Satan can only operate out of the power we provide him. His defeat at Calvary signified our eternal triumph through Jesus Christ.

> And Jesus came and spake unto them, saying, All power is given unto me in heaven and in earth (Matthew 28:18).

> But thanks be to God, which giveth us the victory through our Lord Jesus Christ (I Corinthians 15:57).

Because we are baptized in Christ, we have restored power. The restoration of power illustrates the return of man back to his rightful place of having dominion and authority.

> Genesis 1:26
> And God said, Let us make man in our image, after our likeness: and let them have dominion...

Therefore, we have to begin walking in the authority that we have been given. In Daniel 9:3, 20, -10:11-13, we find Daniel's praying and fasting. He is waiting for the Lord to give him an answer concerning his vision and for his people. However, the scripture tells of a heavenly battle. The prince of Persia held up the messenger with the answer. Because of Daniel's perseverance in prayer and supplications, his answer was released through supernatural intervention. The message of the passage of scripture is two-fold. First, as we make our requests or petitions known unto God no demonic force can prevail against us and win. Prayer pushes through satanic blockages and destroys them. Sometimes our answers are delayed but not denied. Secondly, the character of Daniel is addressed. Daniel was a man who was in right standing with God. He did not defile himself with sin. He was a man dedicated to God and building an open line of communication with God, who was his source of wisdom, strength, and life.

Now, we are partakers of his holiness through Jesus, the mediator of the new covenant who hath broken down the middle wall of partition between us, reconciling us to the father. Jesus Christ is making intercessions for us concerning our request to God. The mystery which in other ages was not made known unto the sons of man, is revealed now unto his holy apostles and prophets by the spirit. For through him we all have access by one spirit unto the Father.

Through Prayer We Recieve Power Over Our Flesh

Prayer gives us the power that allows us to obtain authority over fleshly desires so that we can come into the presence of the Holy God. We will no longer walk after the lust of the flesh but we will walk in the spirit. Prayer gives us the power to lay aside every weight and the sin that would so easily beset us (Hebrews 12: 1). Prayer gives us power to present our bodies as living sacrifice holy and acceptable unto God, which is our reasonable service (Romans 12:1). It has the power to transform our minds allowing us not to be conformed to this world but to be transformed by the renewal of our minds (Romans 12:2). Through prayer, we become committed and submitted to God. Being committed to Him means you change your lifestyle. Your daily living should reflect a life of holiness by being completely obedient to the word and will of God. Prayer is our source of communion with God that we may give Him praise, worship, and adoration. Also, prayer allows us to make our petitions known unto Him. This brings His presence in the midst of our situations giving Him the authority to change the course of the circumstances in our lives.

By inviting his presence, the way is open to allow His divine purpose and plan be fulfilled in us. Although God has absolute authority over all of creation, He will not inject Himself in our lives unless we give Him permission. For example, if you are living in a rented house as long as you pay the note on it every month, the landlord cannot come in any time he wants. Even though it's his house, you are in control, therefore; he needs your permission to enter. In the same sense, this body that you dwell in is not yours, it belongs to God because He has entrusted it to you. You are in control of it. He gave each of us a will and the ability to make choices concerning our lives. He will not force Himself on you against your will. If you ask Him or give Him permission in prayer to take authority in your life, then He will intervene. It is His desire that we should live life in abundance and victoriously through Him.

> Jeremiah 29:11-12 New International Version
> For I know the thoughts I think toward you, says the
> Lord, thoughts of peace and not evil, to give you a
> future and a hope.

> Then when you will call upon me and go and pray to
> me, and I will listen to you.

Through prayer, we receive the anointing of God to break and destroy yokes, bring deliverance in our lives, liberating us from the snares of the devil. Prayer is a compass which helps us to locate our spiritual destination. Prayer helps us discover where we are and determine which way to go, in order to stay in the divine plan of God.

Prayer Teaches Us To Walk In Divine Obedience

Prayer is divine reverence, which causes divine obedience in us. Divine reverence is having deep respect, and love for God, which will make us obedient to His commandments. God is spirit, and his worshipers must worship in spirit and truth (John 4:24 New International Version).

> Philippians 3:3 Amplified Bible
> For we [Christians] are the true circumcision, who
> worship God in spirit and by the Spirit of God and
> exult and glory and pride ourselves in Jesus Christ,
> and put no confidence or dependence [on what we are]
> in the flesh and on outward privileges and physical
> advantages and external appearances

Now the individual who keeps God's commandments abide in Him, and God in him. And by this we know that He abides in us, by the spirit He has given us.

Prayer unlocks the treasures of God, giving us the power and authority we need to reach into the spirit realm and pull down heavenly resources which are the promises of God in to our being. As the sons of God, this is our heritage.

> **Romans 8:14-17**
> **For as many as are led by the Spirit of God, they are the sons of God.**
>
> **For ye have not received the spirit of bondage again to fear; but ye have received the Spirit of adoption, whereby we cry, Abba, Father.**
>
> **The Spirit itself beareth witness with our spirit, that we are the children of God:**
>
> **And if children, then heirs; heirs of God, and joint-heirs with Christ; if so be that we suffer with him, that we may be also glorified together.**

Be anxious for nothing, but in everything by prayer and supplication, with thanksgiving, let your request be made known. And my God shall supply all of your need according to His riches in glory by Christ Jesus (Phil. 4:6&19, Duet. 28:1-14). If you diligently obey the voice of the Lord and observe carefully all His commandments, you will live life abundantly. The Lord will set you high above all the nations of the earth. Blessings shall come upon you and overtake you because you obeyed the voice of the Lord.

THE MODEL PRAYER

The Our Father Prayer is the model prayer. It is the prayer Jesus used to teach us how to pray. The prayer gives us all the elements which are to compose our prayer. For most of us, this just seems like a simple prayer our parents taught us when we were children because it seemed easy a child to learn. This was their way of making sure that we would learn to reverence God. Little did they know, the power that they were passing along. When the prayer is dissected or broken down, we are able to understand its true revelation. Our parents passed to us the most powerful weapon we would ever need. Because of its simplicity most people miss the revelation and power of the model prayer. As I began reading and meditating on it, the Lord began to unfold it to me more. Everything we would ever want to say to God is in this short but powerful prayer. Let us review the prayer.

OUR FATHER When we say Our Father, we are giving the Lord reverence by expressing our eternal unique relationship with Him, as the Father of believers. This is a relationship through grace and a bond established by a covenant through Christ making us (heirs) to the kingdom of God. For you did not receive the spirit of bondage again to fear, but you receive the spirit of adoption by whom we cry "Abba Father" (Romans 8:15).

WHICH ART IN HEAVEN is specifying His location and esteeming Him honor as the creator. Although heaven is His throne where His glory is manifested, it is to the believers a throne of grace. He is not only a father willing to help us but a heavenly father who is able to do exceeding, abundantly above all that we can ask or think.

HALLOW BE THY NAME gives adoration and praise unto Him because He is holy, almighty, all knowing, everlasting, and the eternal Alpha and Omega of the universe. When we praise God, it reflects a true servant's heart. We are praising Him for who He is and for what He does. We are praising Him for His excellent greatness, righteous judgments, eternal love, and extending mercy. By praising Him we are bringing him into the midst of our lives. His word declares that He inhabits our praises; therefore, He dwells in them. Whenever we lift up praise before God, our praises comes up to Him as the smell of incense. This is why is so important to begin our prayers by offering praises of thanksgiving.

THY KINGDOM COME shows we are in anticipation of His arrival to establish His kingdom. We are telling God to allow his kingdom to be manifested in us. We realize that the kingdom of God is righteousness, peace and joy in the Holy Ghost (Romans 14:17). Once we are saved we have become joint heirs to God by the redemptive blood of His son Jesus. This act makes the kingdom available to us. When we say let your kingdom come, we are asking for the dominion of God. We are asking for God to be manifested in us and through us. We are asking Him to rule here on earth and work by saving, delivering, healing or fulfilling whatever petition that has been placed before Him. Once we receive the dominion of God inside of us, we have power and authority to do the same works that Jesus did and even greater works. As believers in Christ, our success depends on the degree of our conformity to His character. We have become transformed through Christ into kingdom. The word of God explicitly explains we are *in* this world but not *of it*. Our citizenship has been divinely changed. We are citizens of heaven. We are to operate here in earth using kingdom principles. We are what the word of God says we are and are equipped to do what the word says we can do to establish the kingdom of God here on earth!

THY WILL BE DONE in this we are surrendering ourselves to God, in complete consecration and dedication that His glory will be revealed through us. We are yielded vessels humbling and submitting our will into His hands. We're asking that He will find favor in us make and trust us to carry His glory. Thy will be done covers a multitude of requests. Our prayers are not selfish and self serving. They evolve to include the will of the Father. The will of God is we, collectively, come to complete obedience to all the laws and ordinances of His will, which shall enable us to do what is pleasing to Him. Our upright walk allows God's will to be manifested in us.

In the natural world, a will is a written, legal declaration of a person's wishes regarding the disposal of his or her property or estate after death. The same can be said about the Bible. The Bible is the written declaration of God's will for us. He left us a multitude of promises some of which are: peace, joy, healing, prosperity, power and authority over situation or circumstance that would arise in our lives. He even sent His son to secure those promises. The shedding of His blood was done on our behalf conquering those things that Satan held captive over us. In taking the keys and power that Satan had obtained from Adam, Jesus made available to us all things. Yet, there are still many of us that do not receive His promises because, we do not have the faith to walk in them or declare them.

We are so natural minded that we limit ourselves to what we see, feel, and what we can obtain in our own limited abilities. Although Satan was left powerless, we are still allowing Him to dictate and control us concerning our abilities to be successful in every life. We are still living beneath our privileges and listening to doubt and fear. This control of Satan makes us look at the circumstance, instead of believing the word. Psalms 24:1 declares "the earth is the Lords and the fullness there of; the world and they that dwell there in". The Psalmist says, "He that hath clean hands and a pure; who hath not lifted up his soul unto vanity, nor sworn deceitfully, shall receive the blessing of the Lord (Psalms 24:4)".

Once we receive him into our hearts, we are no longer servants. We are Sons. As sons, we are legal heirs to the will of God. Once we know His word, and begin to apply it to our lives using the power and authority that is in the name of Jesus, we are able to call those things that are not as though they are. We are able to cause the invisible to manifest and be seen. The only boundaries or limitations we have are those we allow through doubt and disbelief. The promises of God not only refer to natural things but spiritual things, also. I truly believe that eyes have not seen nor ears heard, neither have it entered into the hearts of man the things that God hath prepared for them that love Him (I Corinthians 2:9). God awe is so inspiring that we could never come to an end of knowing

His wonders or his majesty. In order to gain a divine perspective of our lives and receive the will of God, We have to place our souls on the altar before the Lord as a sacrifice and be willing to die to our will. This ultimately means our emotions have to be in alignment with his word.

ON EARTH prays for His will to be established universally. God desires all of humanity to come into agreement and be on one accord working together in harmony for His body to be complete. He wants us to pray that the body of Christ is united with every organ, cell, muscle, bone, and tissue functioning properly regardless of how menial the job seems. He desires that we have peace and harmony on earth to give Him praise of adoration at all times. He desires to show Himself mighty, in all of His majesty, and reveal His glorious wonders to us that we may live life in complete victory.

On Earth refers to allowing His spirit to work in us individually to bring our triune-selves into unity and harmony. In our original makeup, we were created from the dust of the earth and the breath of life blown into us by God. Conclusively, we are simply *living, breathing earth*. Man became a living soul, made of earth and being transformed into flesh to shelter the soul of man; thus, man had a physical form. After God created man He gave man dominion over everything (Genesis 2:7). God desires that man get back into the place with Him that he was in prior to the fall, or better yet, in the beginning (Genesis 1:26). He originally created man to rule on earth in complete lordship, having everything subject to man's authority. Even though man lost that place of power through Jesus, it has been restored. Because of the authority that we have had restored to us whatever we bind or loose on earth, God will confirmed it in heaven.

AS IN HEAVEN refers to all things being in complete harmony and on one accord. All the angels continuously praise and worship Him (Rev. 4:5-11). They are always amazed and marvel at His mighty revelations. They are in complete obedience to His will, which is to give Him praise, honor, and adoration. In Psalms 148:7-10, it states that all creation praises the Lord, because God alone is worthy to be praised.

GIVE US refers to the posture we are to take when making a request. We are to humbly make our request and supplications known. Yes, God has commanded us to ask but there is a manner in which we are to come before him. THIS DAY reminds us that we must live each day as if it were our last. We are to take no thought for tomorrow. We are asking Him at the present time for the necessary provisions needed to sustain us, this day both, naturally and spiritually, so we may walk in victory.

OUR DAILY BREAD: We know that God promised to supply all of our needs according to His riches in glory by Jesus Christ (Philippians 4:19). We also know that man cannot live by bread alone, but by every word that proceedeth out of the mouth of God (Deu. 8:3 and Matt. 4:4). Therefore, we are asking Him to also to crucify us and equip us with the necessary power and weapons for spiritual warfare. We are asking God to teach us his ways and empower us to put off the old man (Colossians 3: 5-10) who grows corrupt by renewing our minds (Romans 12:2) through his holy spirit (Zechariah 4:6). We realize that the weapons of our warfare are not carnal but mighty through God to the pulling down of strongholds, casting down imaginations, and every high thing that exalteth itself against the knowledge of God, bringing into captivity every thought to the obedience of Christ (II Corinthians 10:4). We must put on the whole armor of God that we will be able to withstand in the evil day (Eph. 6:11).

AND FORGIVE US OUR DEBTS we're confessing our wrong deeds and asking Him to blot out our transgressions, and pardon us, so that we can recieve a fresh start. If we confess our sins, He is faithful and just to forgive us our sins and cleanse us from all unrighteousness (I John 1:9).

AS WE FORGIVE to absolve or show mercy to OUR DEBTORS which are those that have wronged or hurt us in some way, whether it was intended or not. Christ became our advocate, although, we were not even worthy. He still loved us and forgave us, even bearing our sins unconditionally. If we are to be His disciples, we have to take on His attributes and have a forgiving heart. If we do not, we will not be forgiven of our sins. We have to love our fellowman and do to them as God does toward us and forgive them unconditionally. He even said,

"How can we say that we love Him whom we've never seen and not love the ones that we dwell among daily?" He said that we would be a liar, it would be impossible to do so. Therefore by loving them, we love God.

AND LEAD US: we are praying for guidance because we're instructed to lean not to our own understanding, but in all our ways to acknowledge Him and He will direct our paths. He said that His word is a lamp unto our feet and a light unto our path (Proverbs 3:5-6 and Psalm 119:105).

NOT INTO TEMPTATION: God knew that we would become prey to all kinds of diverse temptations. He cautions us to stand fast in the liberty wherewith, He has made us free, and be not entangled again with the yoke of bondage (Galatians 5:1). The spirit of the Lord dwelling inside of us, and we are assured that no temptation can overtake us as long as we walk in the Spirit of God. God is faithful, who will not allow us to be tempted beyond what we are able, but will also make the way of escape that we are able to bear it (I Corinthians 10:13).

BUT DELIVER US FROM EVIL: We are asking God to be our salvation, our righteousness, and protection. We're asking come in to our lives and set us free from the bondages of sin, death, and destruction. We ask that He would give us the power we need to lay aside every weight and the sin that would so easily beset us (Hebrews 12:1). As long as we're in our fleshly bodies, we are going to be in a continuous struggle with our flesh but through Christ we will overcome it all. In Christ, we are more than conquers. David wrote, "Behold I was brought forth in iniquity, and in sin my mother conceived me" (Psalm 51:5 New King James Version). We are asking Him to deliver us from the sin nature that was passed down to us from Adam. Through every trial that comes upon us, we are asking Him to forgive us. (Corinthians 12:9) assures us that His grace is sufficient for us and His strength is made perfect in weakness. God said that if we keep our mind on him, he would keep us in perfect peace (Isaiah 26:3). We should ask Him to shield us from the snares of Satan. In I John 2:1 & 2, we learn that if anyone sins, our advocate, Jesus, is righteous. He, himself, is the propitiation for our sins, and not ours only, but for the whole world.

He pleads our case to obtain our forgiveness. (Isaiah 54:17) assures us that no weapon formed against us shall prosper and this is our heritage as being a servant of the Lord. When the enemy comes in like a flood, the spirit of the Lord will lift up a standard against him (Isaiah 59:19). God is our protector.

FOR THINE IS THE KINGDOM, AND THE POWER, AND THE GLORY: We have verbally declared that we are His kingdom representatives, walking in the power of Him and giving Him glory. We are reverencing Him as Lord of all creation and adoring him for his complete dominion in the universe. The Bible states that heaven is His throne and earth is His footstool (Isaiah 66:1). Being that He established the earth this gives Him absolute authority to do with it as He pleases. For we who are the righteous of God are to be established as His kingdom, with His power and His glory being revealed through us.

The Purpose Of Prayer

Prayer was originated as our source of communication with God after the fall of man. It was constructed so that man would realize that he has deficiencies in his life. Originally, man was created in complete perfection, being made in the image of God. After being made in perfection, he was supplied with unlimited resources leaving him without any deficiencies. The Lord planted a Garden Eastward of Eden, and called it The Garden of Eden (Genesis 2:8-24). In Hebrew, "Garden of Eden" means "Delight" or "Garden of Delight." He placed man in it to attend and keep it. Then, God gave him dominion over all. This means that God had given man complete control over everything created and that it would be subject to the authority of man. In this, man was to be God's visible representatives ruling creation as God would. Therefore, man was given the ability to reason, make moral judgments, have freedom of choice, imagination, and unlimited creativity ability. God seeing that man had a need for companionship, God gave him a helper or a companion comparable to him leaving man completely established. As you can see, when God creates, He does it in balance leaving nothing undone.

God left all of creation in the hands of man, whom he gave only one command. God commanded the man saying "of every tree of the garden you may eat freely; but of the tree of the knowledge of good and evil you shall not, eat for in the day that you eat you shall surely die" (Genesis 2:9). Now Satan, being the cunning and crafty strategist, he approached Eve and beguiled her to eat. She then gave it to her husband and he ate also. The act broke the single command given by God.

Although God had warned Adam of the penalty of his disobeying Him, he allowed himself to be deceived and choose to disregard God's warning. Their disobedience plunged the human race into a state of sin and corruption, because of Adam's disobedience they were driven from the garden. This disobedience resulted in man being unclothed of His glory, which was his divine nature that shielded and protected him from death and destruction. From the time man sinned, he was left barren and in need of a way to commune with God. Disobedience moved him out of God's presence, breaking communion with Him.

God is all knowing and in his infinite wisdom he had made man triune. In our make up, we consist of body, soul, and spirit. Our body is the fleshly part of us that shelters the soul and spirit. Our soul is the emotional or conscious part of man that plays the most important role concerning the decisions we make. The spirit part of man is that part of him that would now allow us to be able to communicate with God. God is a spirit and those who worship Him must worship in spirit and in truth. That is why prayer is our way of communicating and communing with God. After the rebellion of one man, Adam, creation was marred. God immediately began to mend it. Now, the whole universe would hinge on the shoulders of one man, His son Jesus.

Disobedience Brings About Destruction

Now man was put out of his place of comfort and placed under judgment. "Cursed is the ground for thy sake, in sorrow shall thy eat of it: all of the days of thy life (Genesis 3:17)." This meant man would realize disobedience opened the door for sin to enter the world and he now has needs. He caused himself to become separated from his creator leaving a void within himself. Even today, it doesn't matter how wealthy a person becomes materialistic. If he has not accepted the Lord as his personal savior, there is a void in his life.

I have listened to some of the most successful people while they were being interviewed. I've often hear them say that through all they have achieved, and with all of their success, there's still a void in their lives. This allows me to believe that no matter how much a person obtains naturally, he will never know complete fulfillment unless his spirit is reconnected to its creator.

When God created man and breathed life into him, He imparted himself in him giving him an unexplainable knowledge of Him. Being that man was the pinnacle of his creation, God gave him godlike attributes along with His eternalness. From the time man sinned, he died spiritually and began dying naturally. Adam was physically placed under the penalty of judgement. "In the sweat of thy face shalt thy eat bread, till thy return unto the ground; for out of it thou was taken: for dust thou art, and unto dust thou shall return" (Genesis 3:19). This left man in need of a way to be restored to his creator. Due to the sin nature, man could no longer commune with God in the state that he had in times before. The sin nature left man with a rebellious spirit that made him arrogant, lustful, and full of pride.

While man was in God, he was clothed with the glory of God. Satan did not have the ability to penetrate man. He knew that only man could break the hedge around himself by making wrong choices. When we accept the Lord Jesus as our personal savior, we are clothed with glory and covered by His blood. For all of you who were baptized in Christ have clothed yourselves with Christ (Gal. 3:27). Therefore, His blood has now become our spiritual hedge. Satan cannot penetrate us no more than we allow him to by ceasing to pray or read the word of God. Satan being a deceitful strategist used another device to beguile man to sin causing death and destruction in humanity. He used the serpent to beguile the woman and the woman to beguile the man to bring about his fall.

The serpent then was the most desirable animal in the animal creation, but now cursed to be the loathsome because he allowed Satan to use Him. The curse of sin didn't only affect the serpent, but also the indwelling energizer, Satan himself. The serpent was cursed more than all the cattle, more than every beast of the field. He was made to go on his belly and eat dust all the days of his life. Too often we make the mistake of misjudging Satan and his tactics when are not being lead by the spirit of God. For the longest, we have been told that if a thing is undesirable it has been compared with or given over to be of the devil. We now know that this is not necessary so. For this purpose, we should watch, as well as, pray to be lead by the spirit of God concerning our lives or everyday decisions. When Satan desires to deceive or destroy us, the object will be very desirable and attractive for his purpose. Being full of the Spirit of God and consistently praying, we will develope discernment and are able to see the trap therefore, we will not fall prey to Satan. Without the spirit of God and constant prayer the opposite occurs.

We become Satan's instrument and are cursed. Satan is able to use us against our brothers in the gospel. He will work in through us to destroy God's people.

> Acts 8:3
> As for Saul, he made havock of the church, entering into every house, and haling men and women committed them to prison.

> Acts 9:1
> And Saul, yet breathing out threatenings and slaughter against the disciples of the Lord, went unto the high priest,

By being used as Satan's instrument, we become cursed. The word plainly tells us to "touch not my anointed and do my prophets no harm" (Psalms 105:15). In Matthew 18:6 (New International Version), we find that it is better to be in the sea with a millstone around our neck than to offend or cause the lest of God's little ones to sin.

Still, Satan's success is in man's fallen state is limited. "I will put enmity between your seed and her seed, He shall bruise your head and you shall bruise his heel." (Genesis 3:15) As we look at this verse it is the first prophecy of the Messiah's coming whose main purpose is to bring humanity back into the presence of God. And when the fullness of time had come, God sent forth His son, born of a woman, born under the law, to redeem them that was under the law, that they might receive the adoption of sons (Gal. 4:4). And the God of peace will crush Satan under your feet (Romans 16:20 Amplified Bible).

God's Providence To Restore Man Back In His Place

God does not move by accident; He moves by providence. He had already prepared the way to restore man. He didn't divest Himself of His deity, but He withheld his preincarnated glory and in humility voluntarily restrict his use of certain attributes and became one of us. God, as the word, explicitly explains he became flesh and dwelt among us. We beheld His glory, as the only begotten of the Father (Romans 4:25). He was delivered up because of our offenses and was raised because of our justification. I Peter 2:9 declares that through Christ, we became as priests being able to enter into the presence of God seeking forgiveness and mercy, and obtaining it. "But ye are a chosen generation, a royal priesthood, a holy nation, a peculiar people that ye should shew forth the praises of Him who hath called you out of darkness into the marvelous light".

He himself is the propitiation for the sins world, by abolishing in his flesh the law with its commandments and regulations. His purpose was to create in himself one new man out of the two, thus making peace. In this one body to reconcile both of them to God through the cross putting to death their hostility. He who knew no sin became sin for us that we might be made the righteousness of

God (II Cor. 5:21). Christ Jesus reunited us to God and gave us the opportunity to come boldly before the throne making our petitions known unto God through his sacrifice. Through salvation, the Holy Spirit can dwells in us making intercessions to the Father in our behalf. So, prayer was design for us to have a way to communicate with God and walk in fellowship with Him daily as priests.

The purpose of prayer is so that we can ask for forgiveness and salvation and we can be eternally justified through our Lord and savior Jesus Christ. As we go in prayer, we are humbling ourselves in humility before God desiring that he will cleanse our souls of all impurities so that we can be intimate with Him. I John 1:9 states that if we confess our sins He's faithful and just enough to forgive us of our sins and cleanse us of all unrighteousness. Before Christ came, we were under the law. The law did not remove sin; instead, it pointed out our failures in doing what God required. Through Jesus, who is our heavenly mediator and advocate, he presents us before the Father pure and blameless. No matter what we've done in the past because of the blood of Jesus our faults never go up before the Lord. Romans 3:24-26 lets us know that now we have been justified freely by His grace through the redemptive blood that is in Christ Jesus. Whom God set forth as a propitiation by His blood, through faith, to demonstrate His righteousness, because in His forbearance God passed over sins that were previously committed.

The purpose of prayer is for mankind to be restored back to our place in God. Every thing that God created, he had a place for it. When God created the waters and the earth, he spoke to the place and commanded it to bring forth the organisms, which were suited to live in the environment. From microscopic diatoms to the great whale, God spoke to the waters and the water brought forth the creatures. Each creature possesses the necessary equipment to live in the aquatic environment. Therefore, when you move a creature from its place, it dies metaphorically and after an extended period of time it will die physically. Removing the fish from the water is dead metaphorically and will eventually lead to the death of the creature. The fish cannot live apart from the water. It is designed to filter oxygen from the water not to breathe oxygen like humans. If you don't soon place it back in some water, it will die naturally.

When God made man He spoke to Himself saying, "let us make man". This key statement attests that man's place was in God. Adam's disobedience moved man out of the presence of God causing him to become dead metaphorically in the spirit, which would result in our dying naturally. Whenever God creates, He creates the spirit first. Then, He brings it into existence in the natural world. Adam's disobedience ushered us into sin leaving us with a debt that we could not pay. It had to be atoned by innocent blood that was unblemished, which we find in Hebrews 9:7, 11-14. The blood of Jesus was unblemished; therefore, it cleansed us from all sin. This gives us the ability to go into the presence of the Holy God.

The purpose of prayer is also for us to worship God giving Him praise because of His sovereignty. We should also give Him praise and worship because of His plan of redemption for us. Even if He never worked another miracle, healed another sick body, or made any more provisions, we would still owe a debt that we could not pay. The shedding of innocent blood purchased our freedom on Calvary and gave us a way of escape from Hell and damnation. We were found guilty of all the charges brought against us. But God loved us so and found worth in us. He sent His son to become the ultimate sacrifice paying an extreme penalty to taste death for every man.

We are all familiar with the fact that He endured much pain and suffering on the cross because we are constantly being made aware His crucifixion. Oft time, we forget Jesus was completely human flesh just like you and me. He had to become one of us in order to be the ultimate sacrifice for sins and redeem us back to the Father. As I go through trails in life, I often think on the crucifixion of Jesus. It helps me to remember that in order to reign with Him, we will have to suffer with Him that we would also be glorified together in Him. Here on earth, we go through some suffering and pains whether it's physical or mental. We always complain and feel that it is beyond our ability to endure it. When praying for healing or deliverance, we are so quick to question the time and not be patient. The issues we deal with can't even begin to be compared to the suffering that Jesus had to endure for us. When we are in pain we have Him to help us bare it. Yet, Jesus had to bear the pain of the cross by himself.

> Matthew 27:46
> And about the ninth hour Jesus cried with a loud
> voice, saying, Eli, Eli, lama sabachthani? that is to say,
> My God, my God, why hast thou forsaken me?

The suffering and pain we are to encounter can not be compared to the anguish Jesus endured on the cross. From his prayer in the Garden of Gethsemane until his ordeal on the cross, Jesus had to withstand the onslaught of Satan's wrath. Jesus could have stopped at any time but he knew that our lives were hanging in the balance. Without a word, Jesus endured the Roman scourging, which tore his flesh to shreds and ultimately left him unrecognizable. The brutality gave us a glimpse of the cruelty and ruthlessness in the heart of man when he is left to himself without God in his life.

Before I began my study of the scourging, I've always heard people say that He only took thirty-nine stripes. After doing research, I learned that He was beaten continuously with a whip known as a flagrum. The flagrum is a long lash comprised of pieces of bones and metal, which would lacerate the flesh of the individual being whipped. If Jesus had been beaten according to the Hebrew customs, he would have been beaten by someone appointed as a lickors. The victim had to be stripped of his clothing, and would receive thirty-nine to forty strips. However, Jesus was whipped according to the Roman customs.

First, Jesus was interrogated by the Roman governor name Pilate. Then, he was given over to the Roman soldiers to be scourged and whipped. The Roman victims were stripped of their clothing and placed at the mercy of their scourgers or licktors. The inflicked wounds exposed the veins, the very muscles sinews, and bowels of the victims. Jesus' scourging surpassed the norm. The reason was He was beaten by Roman soldiers instead of lickors. They were not available. From the crown of His head to the soles of His feet, He was covered with wounds.

After being whipped beyond recognition, He endured the extreme pain of the cross. The actual crucifixion itself was an excruciatingly death in which every nerve in the body cries in pain. To add to the agony, the unnatural position of the body made every movement unbearable. The lacerated veins, the crushed tendons, and the disjointed bones throbbed with incessant pain. Psalms 22:14 stated, "I am poured out like water, my bones are out of joint".

Afore hand, He compared the trauma He would embrace with the grief of a woman in child birth. This is not to say that our pain in giving birth is as terrible as His. It is only way to compare joy of seeing and holding the new baby and the relief the pain is over. Jesus knew he was to enter into a state of tremendous pain and suffering, this is why He said if it be my will, I will that this cup be passed from me. Nevertheless not my will but thine will. Because the disciples were devoted to him they would mourn and be in sorrow. Yet, only for a little while.

> Psalm 30:5
> … weeping may endure for a night, but joy cometh in
> the morning.

They would grieve and mourn while the world rejoiced, but when it was finished their grief would turn to joy because His purpose was accomplished.

As the Roman soldiers whipped His body, every strip not only bruised his flesh but it broke open his flesh. The breaking of His flesh was our way to receive healing in ours. Every sickness known to humanity was being laid on Him. While He was being whipped the nations were being healed, also. Isaiah 53:5 declares:

> He was wounded for our transgressions (our
> disobedience), bruised for our iniquities (sins,
> wickedness or wrong doings). The chastisement of
> our peace was upon Him, "discipline or regulations of
> our minds and harmony within us, and to bring unity
> between us by breaking down the barriers of traditions
> such as the demon of religiosity in the body of Christ.
> With His stripes, we are healed, restored back in His
> presence, and nursed back to health.

Not only were we healed in our personal bodies, this was done for the healing of the universal body of Christ. II Chronicles 7:14 states:

> If my people who are called by my name would
> humble themselves and pray and seek my face and turn
> from there wicked ways, then will I hear from heaven, I
> will forgive their sins and heal their lands.

According to Isaiah 53:2, there was no beauty in Him that we should desire. This meant Jesus' external appearance was marred. His beard was pulled, punched in the face, and spit on left him unrecognizable. It was unpleasing to the eye to look unto his countenance. Moreover, this refers to the fact that there was no beauty in His message and His purpose for being here as the Son of God.

He was breaking down the traditions and cultures differences of highly respectable religious people. He was the Son of God on assignment from the Father; yet, He was ridiculed and cast down. His own people did not receive him because He was in this world but not of it (Isaiah 53:3). He was despised and rejected by men. A man of sorrows acquainted with grief. We hid as it was our faces from Him. He was despised and we esteemed him not. To make this more incredible, while we were His enemies, Jesus still chose to endure the afflictions of being beaten, ridiculed, ostracized, and even the suffering death on the cross for our sake. In this God demonstrated His love toward us while we were yet sinners. This is why He says that there is no greater love than the love of one who would lay his life down for a friend (John 15:13).

It is necessary to pray that we might know purpose. Once you know your purpose, you won't be easily defeated. The purpose of prayer is to provide strength to overcome the world as Jesus did. I believe that in everything that He suffered from the time of his being carried before the governor until his resurrection from the grave to his ascension in to the heavens had purpose. Any individual who has a sense of purpose has an identity. When purpose and identity are united, then, the individual will seek out his destiny to fulfill it.

In the Old Testament, the allusions to the *face* speak of physical conditions or strength. Therefore, the blood shed from His face was for our strength that we might remain strong in the Lord when we have been commissioned by Him or a set apart. When we are going through trials and tribulations, being persecuted, we should remain strong and be determined that nothing will separate us from the love of God (Romans 5:3,4) Knowing that tribulations produces perseverance, and perseverance character and character hope. When our hope is in the Hope of glory, we know that we are more than conquers through Him that loved us. All things are working together for the good to those who love the Lord and who are called according to His purpose (Romans 8:28). II Corinthians 12:9 reminds us that God's grace is sufficient for [us], for My strength is made perfect in weakness. This means when you have come to the end of your personal strength, you will find the beginning of Him or His strength. God is there all the time, but most of the time He can't begin to work for us until we reach the end of ourselves.

When the crown of thorns was placed on His head, the thorns pierced his skull. The piercing signified deliverance in our minds and the giving of authority over our thoughts, so that we can take on the mind of Christ (Romans 12:6). Understandable the old man was crucified with Him that the body of sin might be done away with that we should no longer be slaves of sin which gives us the ability to not to be conformed to this world, but to be transformed by the renewal of our minds through Christ Jesus (Romans 12:2). This renewal is to come especially through prayer to God in everything.

> Be anxious for nothing, but in everything by prayer
> and supplications, with thanksgiving, let your request
> be known to God (Phil. 4:6).

This transformation is a life long process that will not be completed until we are with Christ. We can be confident that the work that He has begun in us will complete it until the day of Jesus Christ (Phil. 1:6). As they were taking Him up to Golgotha, the soldiers commanded a man named Simon to help Jesus carry. This is symbolic of us carrying our burdens. When the load is too heavy and hard for us to carry, Jesus steps in and carries them for us.

While He became sin for us being stretched out on the cross his bones were being pulled out of joint and his heart almost erupted from the pressure that was being applied. Jesus not only suffered the physical pain but the spiritual pressure as well. He not only felt the pressure from being stretch in that position of carrying the cross but the pressure of us, weight of the sins of humanity. There are times when trails have us stretched out of measure feeling that we are being pulled apart. Through the power of prayer and the spirit of God, we are held together.

> Reproach has broken my heart, I am full of heaviness;
> I looked for someone to take pity but there was none
> (Psalms 69:20).

The blood shed from the piercing of His hands was done so that we would not have to work for salvation. Through Jesus' work at Calvary, He eternally paid the price and made salvation a gift. All we have to do to receive the gift of salvation is to ask and believe in Him. As I said before salvation for us is free but it was not cheap. It cost God his only Son and cost Jesus His life. Without the shedding of Jesus' blood, there would never have been remission of sin. Therefore, as through one man's offense, judgment came to all men, resulting in condemnation, even so through one man's righteous act the free gift of came to all men, resulting in justification of life (Romans 5:18, 10:9-10).

> For the wages of sin is death, but the gift of God is
> eternal life in Christ Jesus our Lord (Romans 6:23).

The blood oozing from His feet was for our walk, so that we might walk in this world but not be a part of it. When we are not entangled with the things of this world, and our message is not compromising with the world. There are going to be times that you will find yourself being rejected and undesirable in the eyes of humanity. There will be times when you will have to stand alone without family or peers. John 15:18-19 states, "If the world hates you, you know that it hated me (Christ) before it hates you". If you were of the world, the world would love its own. Because you are not of the world, but I chose you out of the world, therefore the world hates you (Matt.27:50, 51;Mark 15:37,38; Luke 23:45,46; John 19:30). When Jesus cried out in a loud voice, I believed that He was dismissing his spirit from his body. Being that He had walked in complete perfection, death had no power over him. Jesus declared, "No man take my life, but I willingly laid it down. The veil of the temple was torn from top to bottom when Jesus had made atonement for our sins. This made it possible for us to go into the presence of God without the priest. We all became as priests being able now to petition God for ourselves. He loosed the reins of sin and death over humanity (Matt. 27:52, 53).

In that day, it was tradition for them to break the legs of an individual to confirm their death or to speed it up. Exodus 12:46, Num.9:12, and Psalms 22:16,17, says that because of the prophecies that went forth concerning that death of the Messiah, that there was not to be a bone broken. Although they broke the legs of the other men that was crucified, they did not break His leg. In this Jesus represented the body of saints being restored to the father. When we come forth as the body of Christ we are to be whole and in complete perfection. When Jesus was pierced in His side it was symbolic to his giving birth to us spiritually as the blood and water came from it. As Adam side was open giving birth to the first creation, bringing forth Eve. Jesus side was open giving spiritual birth to us bringing us into the newness of life thus restoring us back to the Father. We all know that in giving birth the water breaks first then the blood follows. Even in doing this Jesus worked a miracle on the cross because when the body dies everything becomes stilled and it is impossible for blood and water to run from our bodies after death is complete. Jesus did this being the second Adam He had to give the second birth to creation thus, bringing forth purity, and cleansing for us as He became our sin offering. The blood represented redemption and the water represented the spirit being shed abroad in us.

Jesus Victory Beyond The Cross

In his pure Human spirit He had to descend into the lowest Hell (Ephesians 4:9, Acts 2:22-31) enduring all the pain humanity would suffer. For the first time, Jesus experienced total separation from the Father. He was given over completely to Satan's tactics in a place of torment where all impenitent sinners were imprisoned upon leaving this life (Acts 2: 22-31). His endurance in the dark prison is believed to be described in Psalms 88.

> He (The Father) laid Him in the lowest pit of the underworld, in the dark place, in dense darkness. I (Jesus) am full of trouble, weighted with evils. Thou hast brought me to Shoel, the kingdom of death. I am a man without God. Thy wrath lie hard upon me, Thy wrath passeth, thou laid thy fury upon me. Thy has afflicted me with thy waves. I have called upon thee day and night and thou hearest me not. I have borne thy terrors so that I am distracted helpless. The outburst of thy wrath , thy streams of wrath cut me off.

No finite mind can fully comprehend the dept of anguish He endured. Perhaps Isaiah described it best in verse 53:12. He wrote that He had poured out His soul unto death. Jesus suffered in our stead until the mind of God and the claims of eternal justice were fully met. The pleasure of the Lord shall prosper in His hand. He shall see the travail of His soul and be satisfied. When we take all this into consideration, we still cannot begin to comprehend the measure of the Father's love for us in giving His only Son knowing what He would have to suffer for our sake. Neither can we began to understand the Son's desire to please His Father in knowing what was ahead yet choosing to drink the bitter cup of woe. Jesus consciously decided to allow himself to be completely forsaken of the Father's love in order to provide full atonement for all of humanity! We deserved death but love provided mercy. While Jesus prayed in the Garden of Gethsemane, it was his human nature which desired that the cup be passed from him because he knew what lie ahead (Matt. 26:39. He knew that man even in his sinful, backslidden, and dying state was still the pinnacle of God's creation and God loved man. Therefore, Jesus consented and replied by the help of his spiritual strength, "Nevertheless not my will but thine will".

When we pray, it is important to ask God to teach us how to be submissive to His will and give us the power to resist the temptations of the flesh. Submissiveness makes it easier to say from our hearts not my will but your will be done in our lives. For most of us, the battle in our flesh will be the hardest battle that we will ever fight. Because the flesh is Satan's main target of attack, it is necessary for us to stay in the presence of God continuously asking God crucify our flesh. When most people talk about crucifying the flesh, they tend to make it sound so easy. Consequently, it is not. In Roman 7, Paul provides a wonderful description of the attack in the flesh.

Roman 7:22-25

For I endorse and delight in the Law of God in my
inmost self [with my new nature].

But I discern in my bodily members [in the sensitive
appetites and wills of the flesh] a different law (rule of
action) at war against the law of my mind (my reason)
and making me a prisoner to the law of sin that dwells
in my bodily organs [in the sensitive appetites and
wills of the flesh].

O unhappy and pitiable and wretched man that I am!
Who will release and deliver me from [the shackles of]
this body of death?

O thank God! [He will!] through Jesus Christ (the
Anointed One) our Lord! So then indeed I, of myself
with the mind and heart, serve the Law of God, but
with the flesh the law of sin.

Because there is always a war going on in the flesh, some will
say all it takes is a made up mind and that is true to an extent.
However, you must be endowed with the power of the Holy Spirit.
In order to walk in the spirit, you have pray, stay in the word of
God and even fast that God will give you power to stand. When you
are in a battle with Satan and his demonic forces, you are battling
in the spirit realm. In order to win, you have to be equipped with
spiritual weapons, which are given to us through prayer.

> For the weapons of our warfare can not be carnal but
> mighty in God for pulling down strongholds, casting
> down imaginations, and every high thing that exalt
> itself against the knowledge of God, bringing every
> thought into captivity to the obedience of Christ (Cor.
> 10:4-5).

Before engaging in spiritual warfare, you must have on the whole armor of God that you may be able to stand against the schemes of the devil (Eph. 6:12-18).

> For we wrestle not against flesh and blood, but
> against principalities, against powers, against rulers
> of darkness of this age, against a host of spiritual
> wickedness in heavenly places.

We have to have our loins gird about with the truth, put on the breastplate of righteousness, which means to literally "put on Jesus". Having our feet shod with the preparation of the gospel of peace, "to walk in humility, follow peace with all men". We must ready to give an answer to everyone who asks you a reason for the hope that is in you with meekness and fear. We must take the shield of faith that we may be able to quench the fiery darts of the wicked one. As Christians, we are to put on the helmet of salvation and carry the sword of the spirit, which is the word of God. The way that we dress in the armor is through prayer. In the end, the purpose of prayer is to properly prepare us for warfare that we may walk in victory and in the authority that belongs to us.

His Victory Was Not Only Legal It Was Dynamic

Justice demanded not only the turning over God's son to Satan but the full measure of the Father's wrath against all cumulated sin of the human race had to be poured upon Jesus. In this, He was completely justified that all power in the heaven above and in earth below was to come subject to the authority of the name Jesus. Through everything He endured for humanity's sake in order to please the Father redeeming and restoring us back to Him, Jesus earned the honor to be in His place of power and glory at the right hand of the Father. His victory was not only legal, it was dynamic. Everything that Satan done to prevent the plan of God for our redemption and to keep us as slaves to sin was turned around for our good. When God has a plan for our lives if we trust Him and continue to pray and seek him diligently, the design will come to past. Sin now has no more dominion over you. Being made free from sin ye became servants of rightousness. He legally accepts a repenting sinner and makes him a member of His of His universal family. You must learn to take all of your problems to God regardless to their nature, because He is interested in all of your problems.

Therefore, if by chance you fell or find yourself in a backslidden state, I would like to make an appeal. I invite you to repent, get up, and get back in the race for God. The race is not given to the swift nor the battle to the strong (Ecc. 9:11)but to the ones that endure until the end (James 5:11). Sometimes you have to think of yourself as a baby, then, a child growing and occasionally making mistakes.

Later, we mature into a productive adults, who have become seasoned with grace, wisdom and understanding. When a baby first starts to walk, they always stumble. Walking is a new experience. The idea of how to balance the body and remain steady is new! There are times that they get so excited about the fact that they are walking; they move to fast and fall. After accepting Christ into your heart, you must allow yourself to be nourished properly. It is the study of word, coupled with prayer are you able to reduce the times you fall or stumble.

As babies grow up, we give them all the basic fundamentals that they need to be self sufficient. When we receive salvation, this is a new experience. We are now babes in Christ; therefore, we need someone to instruct us in how to balance ourselves by giving us the word of God and teaching us how to pray. If we don't reject the teaching, we will properly develop to become productive Christians. Still, along with teaching comes training. Training is a process that requires time. In our walk with Christ, we learn how to pray, get understanding of the word of God, how to witness effectively, and how to allow the spirit of God to operate in us with the gifts. If we don't remain steadfast in the will of God we will continue to stumble and error.

Overtime, I have found that some who have been converted become arrogant. This seems to come about as the spirit of God begins to refine. In some, I have noticed pride. They exalt themselves and try to move ahead of their leadership. Although you may feel like you are ready to take on the world don't be deceived. Pray that God will discipline your spirit and give you a teachable heart to always respect authority. When He has placed you under a leader, no matter how much zeal you feel, you must wait to be released by your leader. Remember Samuel and Eli. Although Samuel heard the call of the Lord, he did not answer the call until Eli instructed him to do so. After which, the ministry of Samuel the Prophet began to manifest.

> I Samuel 3:7-9
> Now Samuel did not yet know the LORD, neither was the word of the LORD yet revealed unto him.
>
> And the LORD called Samuel again the third time. And he arose and went to Eli, and said, Here am I; for thou didst call me. And Eli perceived that the LORD had called the child.
>
> Therefore Eli said unto Samuel, Go, lie down: and it shall be, if he call thee, that thou shalt say, Speak, LORD; for thy servant heareth. So Samuel went and lay down in his place.

When it is your time to move to the next level or leave their ministry God will allow them to know. Most assuredly, Satan will come to attack in your area of growth but be equipped to fight.

Regardless of your reason for your fall, the important thing is your return to Jesus. Repent and ask for forgiveness. He is so merciful and kind. No matter what we have done in the past, He's willing to forgive us and accept us back. Whatever you do don't allow public opinions or self pride to keep you from to God. Allow the potter to place you back on the wheel and create a new vessel out of you. Let God refine you to bring out the inner treasure in you , which is the beauty of Him inside you.

RESOURCES

Gospel Communications International. (2006). BibleGateway. com. Referenced sources using the online Amplified and King James Bibles.

The Holy Bible Old & New Testament in King James Version. (1976). Nashville: Thomas Nelson Publishers.

The Open Bible: The New King James Version (1990). Nashville: Thomas Nelson Publishers.

Student Bible: New International Version. (1992) Grand Rapids: The Zondervan Corporation Publishers.

Packer, J. I., Merrill, C. T, and White, W. (1995). Nelson's Illustrated Encyclopedia of Bible Facts: A comprehensive fact-finding sourcebook on all the people, places, and customs of the Bible. Nashville: Thomas Nelson Publishers.

Youngblood, R. F., Bruce, F. F., and Harrison R. K. (1995). New Illustrated Bible Dictionary: Completely revised and updated edition. Nashville: Thomas Nelson Publishers.

About the Author

Olivia Daniels-Pierce is the daughter of the late Minister Leo and Mother Lorene Daniels. She was born and reared in North Carolina and is the fourth child of nine children. Of her eight siblings, she was a peculiar child. She matriculated through the North Carolina Public School System. Olivia further her studies at Cathedral Bible College in Myrtle Beach, South Carolina, where she has earned her associates and bachelor degrees.

After being raised in a God-fearing environment, she accepted Christ as her savior at a young age. She was taught how to pray for God's divine help and instruction for various situations and circumstance occurring in her home, school, and her personal life.

Later in life, she married. Olivia is the proud mother of four daughters: Vaccarol, Regina, Melissa, and Danielle, and one son, Mekel. Having a family of her own she began to experience that there was more to prayer than just words. She realized that through the baptism of the Holy Spirit, prayer bring manifestation, revelation, along with experience. It is through prayer that one can enter into the very presence of God.

The anointing of prayer in her life inspired her to write this book. The Power of Prayer was written to explain the dimensions of prayer that allows believers to communicate on an intimate level with God, which in turn moves God.

Olivia is an anointed intercessor, who "battles" for the saints of God through prayer. Her passion is for souls to be saved and have an understanding that daily prayer is a necessity. For it is through prayer we communicate with God.

www.ingramcontent.com/pod-product-compliance
Lightning Source LLC
Chambersburg PA
CBHW031303060726
47590CB00003B/1035